NOTHING IS HIDDEN

THE PSYCHOLOGY
OF
ZEN KOANS

NOTHING IS HIDDEN

THE PSYCHOLOGY OF
ZEN KOANS

BARRY MAGID

WISDOM PUBLICATIONS • BOSTON

Wisdom Publications
199 Elm Street
Somerville, MA 02144 USA
www.wisdompubs.org

Library of Congress Cataloging-in-Publication Data
Magid, Barry.
 Nothing is hidden : the psychology of Zen koans / Barry Magid.
   pages cm
 Includes bibliographical references and index.
 ISBN 1-61429-082-2 (pbk. : alk. paper)
 1. Zen Buddhism—Psychology. 2. Koan. I. Title.
 BQ9265.8.M34 2013
 294.3'927—dc23
                            2013000339

ISBN 978-1-61429-082-7
eBook ISBN 978-1-61429-102-2

17 16 15 14 13
5 4 3 2 1

Cover design by Phil Pascuzzo. Interior design by Gopa&Ted2, based on a design by DC Design. Set in Sabon LT Std 10.5/15.5. Author photo by Peter Cunningham.

"Song in the Manner of Housman" by Ezra Pound, from COLLECTED EARLY POEMS, copyright ©1976 by The Ezra Pound Literary Property Trust. Reprinted by permission of New Directions Publishing Corp.

Wisdom Publications' books are printed on acid-free paper and meet the guidelines for permanence and durability of the Production Guidelines for Book Longevity of the Council on Library Resources.

Printed in the United States of America.

This book was produced with environmental mindfulness. We have elected to print this title on 30% PCW recycled paper. As a result, we have saved the following resources: 12 trees, 6 million BTUs of energy, 1,064 lbs. of greenhouse gases, 5,770 gallons of water, and 380 lbs. of solid waste. For more information, please visit our website, www.wisdompubs.org. This paper is also FSC® certified. For more information, please visit www.fscus.org.

IN MEMORIAM
Charlotte Joko Beck
(1917–2011)

CONTENTS

INTRODUCTION

Both as a student and a teacher, I have had a complicated relationship to koans, one that perhaps mirrors many of the twists and turns of their use in America. As a Dharma heir of Charlotte Joko Beck, I belong to a Zen lineage that contains elements of both Rinzai and Soto practices, the two primary traditions of Japanese Zen. Rinzai Zen is usually identified with koan practice; the student typically starts with a initial koan like Mu and then moves through a sequence of koans centered on the canonical collections, among which are the Gateless Gate and the Blue Cliff Record, which were assembled almost one thousand years ago. Soto Zen is grounded in *shikantaza* or "just sitting," a form of practice established in Japan by Eihei Dogen in the thirteenth century. Dogen also used koans—or at least gave numerous talks based on koans—but teachers in the Soto lineages typically did not use them in the systematic, question-and-answer way that characterized the Rinzai lineages as revived by the renowned master Hakuin in eighteenth-century Japan.

Although there are pure Rinzai and Soto lineages in America, the lineage I belong to is a hybrid of the two, as indeed are most Zen lineages in America. This fact is largely due to the influence of a single remarkable teacher, Hakuun Yasutani (1885–1973). Yasutani started off as monk in the Soto Zen tradition, studying under a teacher who was considered one of the greatest Dogen scholars of his day, Nishiari Bokusan. But as a young monk, Yasutani was disillusioned by what he saw as the complacency of his fellow monks.

Their great founder Eihei Dogen (1200–1253) had taught that Zen meditation was not a means to an end, not a technique for achieving enlightenment, but that practice and realization were inseparably one and the same. Dogen wrote, "The zazen I speak of is not meditation practice. It is simply the Dharma gate of joyful ease, the practice-realization of totally culminated enlightenment."

However, Yasutani thought that what he saw around himself in the monastery was neither joyful nor enlightened and that the true spirit of Dogen was missing from Nishiari's Zen. His condemnation of his teacher was harsh:

> Beginning with Nishiari Zenji's, I have examined closely the commentaries on the Shobogenzo [Dogen's masterwork] of many modern people, and though it is rude to say it, they have failed badly in their efforts to grasp its main points. . . . It goes without saying that Nishiari Zenji was a priest of great learning and virtue, but even a green priest like me will not affirm his eye of *satori* [enlightenment]. . . . So it is my earnest wish to correct to some degree the evil [of Nishiari's theoretical Zen] in order to requite his benevolence, and that of his disciples, which they have extended over many years.

Yasutani left Nishiari's monastery, married, and became an elementary school teacher. He nonetheless continued his practice with a number of different teachers—until he met Harada Sogaku Roshi. Harada also had been a Soto priest, whose own search had brought him to study with Toyota Dokutan (1841–1919), abbot of Nanzenji, a Rinzai temple. Harada completed koan study with him and become his Dharma successor, though he formally remained a Soto priest, eventually becoming abbot of Hosshinji, a Soto temple. Yasutani sat his first sesshin with Harada in 1925 and two years later at the age of forty-two was recognized as having attained *ken-sho*, an initial experience of enlightenment. Ten years later, at the age of fifty-eight, he finished his koan study and received Dharma transmission from Harada Roshi on April 8, 1943.

Yasutani first came to the United States in 1962, at the invitation of Philip Kapleau, who had studied with Harada Roshi at Hossinji. Kapleau, whose book *The Three Pillars of Zen* introduced many of my generation of Americans to Zen practice, went on to be the founder of the Rochester Zen Center. Other students of Yasutani were Robert Aitken and Taizan Maezumi, each of whom went on to establish flourishing American lineages. Yet while I would eventually train and receive Dharma transmission in Charlotte Joko Beck's branch of the Yasutani-Maezumi lineage, my first experience of Zen was with the Rinzai teacher Eido Shimano, whose own mixture of charisma, insight, and sexual misconduct provided a whole generation of American Zen students with their first true koan. In many important ways, this and my previous books have been attempts to keep working on that first koan: the relationship of realization to personal character and psychology, how the two intersect, or how, all too often, they can instead be like two arrows missing in midair.

When I came to New York City in 1975, after medical school, to begin my residency training in psychiatry, I began looking for an analyst and looking for a place to begin practicing Zen. Eido's Zen Studies Society appeared to be the only game in town as far as Zen went; the options for psychoanalytic training were far more diverse and complicated.

In those days, it felt like my psychoanalytic world was divided into two camps, the followers of Heinz Kohut and the followers of Otto Kernberg. The world of psychoanalysis was obviously far more complex than that, with Freudians, Kleinians, Sullivanians, Horneyans, Jungians, and Winnicottians all competing for attention—not to mention the popular nonanalytic offshoots of Gestalt and Transactional Analysis.

Kohut was famous for advocating an empathic stance by the analyst as an alternative to the classical Freudian "blank screen" neutrality. He thought of people's struggles in terms of their frustrated, healthy, arrested developmental strivings for love and attention. Otto Kernberg, on the other hand, stressed the role of primitive aggression and thought that, deep down, patients were trying to destroy the analyst, driven by uncontrollable envy and a need to split their emotional world into competing all-good and all-bad factions. Although I was drawn to Kohut's picture, I nonetheless found myself enacting the Kerbergian drama by casting Kernberg himself as the psychoanalytic equivalent of Darth Vader to Kohut's Obi Wan Kenobi. Kohut and Kernberg were, each after his own fashion, pioneers in the treatment of narcissistic and borderline personality disorders, both of which were characterized by a sense of inner emptiness and depression, an unstable sense of self, often wildly alternating between grandiosity and worthlessness, and chronically difficult personal relationships. The borderline did the narcissist one better by being in a more chronic state of anger and resentment at how others were treating or neglecting him; the narcissist's grandiosity holding up a slightly more stable, if brittle, shield against the world.

With great reluctance, and not a little anxiety, I had to admit that I saw most of this in the mirror every morning.

Kohut represented some hope for people like me, while Kernberg offered only the grim caveat that individuals with these sorts of personality disorders, while potentially treatable, were clearly unsuited to be therapists themselves. "What if I am a borderline?" was the question that kept nagging at the back of my mind as I began my career as a psychiatrist and my own analytic training. That conclusion was simultaneously unacceptable and inescapable. It served as a nexus for all my self-doubt, all my self-hate, all my fears that my professional self was a sham and that deep down I was crazy. Whether, as a beginning psychiatrist, my self-diagnosis was accurate or not is beside the point. (Medical students are notorious for imagining they have contracted every disease they are studying.) The question roiled my guts and made my mind reel with endlessly inconclusive arguments pro and con. Without my realizing it, that question was my first koan.

One day—and I can still remember it some thirty-five years later—as I was walking across Union Square Park, about to catch the subway to go to see my analyst—I suddenly gave up. "Alright, I'm a borderline. That's it." Amazingly, instead of being plunged into the despair and hopelessness I always thought this conclusion would entail, to say nothing of the impending collapse of my psychiatric career, I felt an enormous burden had been lifted. I was no longer fighting with myself, I was no longer trying to ward off or deny some part of my self that had me terrified.

The traditional Zen koans offer us the chance to encounter and reengage what we consciously or unconsciously consider "not-me." Sometimes, as in my case, it will be a part of me that is considered damaged, shameful, or incongruent with the person I am trying to be. But there is a much wider range of self-experience from which we may be cutting ourselves off. We may deny or try to minimize our animal nature, striving to be rational rather than emotional, in control rather than vulnerable to the vicissitudes of life. We may attempt to deny our very mortality and try to make what we call the "spiritual" into a portal into another, perhaps immortal, life, beyond death. We may deny the part of ourselves that is interconnected and dependent on others, seeking autonomy and stoic self-sufficiency. And finally, we may cut ourselves off from our own intrinsic wholeness and perfection, idealizing teachers or buddhas whom we imagine are utterly and qualitatively different from ourselves, beings of another order, whose attainments never can really be fully our own.

The way in which I will use not just "personal" koans like this but traditional ones as well to engage and work through psychological impasses may strike some of those trained in the traditional methods of koan study as illegitimate, superficial, trivializing—or all of the above. When I began my Zen training, reference to what was "psychological" was almost always prefaced by "the merely." Zen went "deeper" than that. Koans were considered to be Zen's unique key to breaking through to the "Absolute." The sitting cushion—the *zafu*—not the analyst's couch, was where one would find true liberation from the self. Yet the fruits of those breakthroughs, the promised liberation from the suffering self, proved far more elusive and much less transformative of day-to-day character than advertised.

It turned out that even the seemingly most intense transcendent experiences faded and their afterglow did not so reliably trickle down into the recesses of our unconscious minds. More and bigger realizations were not by themselves the answer. Not only did realization fail to heal the deep divisions in our character, more and more it looked as if for many people, and in particular for many Zen teachers, practice opened up bigger and bigger splits between an idealized compassionate self and a shadow self, where split off and denied sexual, competitive, and narcissistic fantasies held sway.

Although the traditional koan system was touted as being designed precisely to bring one down from the hundred foot pole of pernicious oneness (the use of spiritual experiences of any kind to remain "above it all") its capacity to engage and work through character disorder in light of and within the crucible of realization turned out to be severely limited. In psychological terms, one would say that though it delivered on the promise of insight, it failed in the process of working through, of integrating realization with our deeply ingrained character styles. It is that failure of working through that I hope to address in this work. My own teacher, Joko Beck, declared that koans simply failed to address emotion in any meaningful and systematic way. She was speaking from experience, and she was no doubt correct in her assessment, given her teacher's extraordinary proficiency at teaching koans and his equally extraordinary personal failings as a human being. I do not use koans in the traditional manner of dokusan presentation. Instead, I have tried to open up their imagery the way I would with a dream and make that imagery emotionally evocative and illuminating of the underlying psychological splits that need to be engaged if realization is to actually penetrate all facets of our personality.

As Zen students we can indeed achieve moments in which our everyday dualistic boundaries between the self and the world would seem to dramatically dissolve—and yet it turns out that the dualisms that matter most in our lives are more persistent, more elusive, and more unconsciously engrained.

Ordinary Mind used Heinz Kohut's self psychology as its psychoanalytic organizing theory. This book will expand on that conceptual base by including a broader *relational* analytic perspective, particularly Philip Bromberg's work on dissociation, as well as Jessica Benjamin on intersubjectivity, Emmanuel Ghent on submission and surrender, and attachment theory as grounded in the work of John Bowlby and Mary Ainsworth.

Graham Greene, in the epigraph to his first novel, *Brighton Rock*, illustrates one aspect of the phenomena this expanded perspective attempts to address: "There's another man within me, and he's angry with me." The other man within—simultaneously someone who is both my self and not me; someone who is judging me by a set of standards that are not quite my own, not quite available to my own scrutiny, but which I also cannot escape. Note how different Greene's declaration is from the simple statement "I am angry with myself." Being angry with one's self reflects a more ordinary sense of conflict, of, say, not having done what one knows would have been the right thing to do. But to have "another man within" reflects the more mysterious phenomenon of dissociation, of having one part of one's self being *other* to another part. Dissociation, being cut off emotionally from aspects of ourselves that feel like "not-me," whether our vulnerability, our sexuality, our aggression, our need for love, our sense of inner damage or inner wholeness, are the dualisms of everyday life that create the suffering that practice is meant to relieve.

As I have discussed in my previous books, these splits within our self are the most painful manifestation of dualism in our lives. In Buddhist jargon, dualism too easily becomes a metaphysical abstraction, a philosophical whipping boy that we can all agree represents a false dichotomization of reality, a delusional perspective that we pay lip service to disavowing.

This all-too-glib dismissal of dualism ignores both its tenacious unconscious roots as well as its ubiquitous place in organizing our everyday experience.

Thus, on the one hand, we remain unaware of how the dissociative aspects of dualism split off our emotional from our spiritual lives, and on the other, we maintain a guilty relationship to all the complex ways we individually, culturally, and politically organize our experience using dualistic frames of reference, such as male and female, self and other, family and strangers, likes and dislikes, enlivening work and soul-killing drudgery, and so on. We should also bear in mind the insight of Simone de Beauvoir that all the famous dualisms of Western history could be seen as arising out of the opposition of male and female, and that all the masculine sides of the polarity (authority, strength, agency) were valued, while all those seen as feminine (dependency, vulnerability, passivity) were devalued. Inequalities of gender, income, and power are not dichotomies that exist only in our imagination and that can be dissolved in a personal spiritual experience on the cushion. These inequalities have been culturally grafted onto Buddhism over many centuries in Asia and are only now being questioned as it is being transplanted in America.

My primary concern in this book, however, will be how our individual meditation practice can be distorted by unexamined psychological processes that enlist traditional concepts like dualism into the service of our unconscious defensive agendas. For example, I have seen Buddhist practitioners exert great efforts to eliminate any trace of preference for comfort over discomfort in their lives, while ignoring a pervasive unconscious underlying belief that others, but not they themselves, are entitled to love, care, or happiness.

In the chapters that follow, I will explore the psychological mechanisms of denial, dissociation, and idealization that foster these kinds of splits. I will do so from the theoretical and clinical perspective of a psychoanalyst, which, in tandem with Zen, is how I've worked and practiced all my professional life. I realize that for some readers, psychoanalysis may represent a seemingly interminable old-fashioned therapeutic approach that is rapidly being overtaken by short-term cognitive-behavioral techniques. It is not my intention to debate the relative merits of different therapeutic approaches here—rather, I hope to illustrate what a psychoanalytic understanding can bring to the intersection of Zen practice and personal psychology and let that presentation stand or fall on its own merits.

I will try to show how the vivid imagery of koans can offer us a metaphorical way to engage the splits in our psyche and how they point to a reengagement with the whole of ourselves, a wholeness far greater and more encompassing than we ever imagined. My choices do not follow any standard sequence, nor are they meant to be in any way a comprehensive guide to traditional koan study. With the exception of Mu, I have tried to choose koans that I did not discuss in my previous books. If my interpretations sometimes stray from the traditional path, so be it. Given the choice, I prefer to "make it new" (in Ezra Pound's words) rather than to follow along well-worn paths, where many other, more traditional guides are available.

CHAPTER ONE

WHOLENESS & IMMEDIACY

"THAT'S ME."

Psychoanalysis begins with Freud's discovery of the unconscious, an unconscious that he postulated was filled with thoughts, fantasies, and wishes so upsetting to our ordinary conscious mind that they must be repressed.

Buddhism, on the other hand, begins with Shakyamuni's experience of wholeness and perfection, a realization that what we deny ourselves is not just a vision of the forbidden and frightening side of human nature but of its wonder as well. Within the broader cultural context of Zen in America, the two traditions all too often have failed to interact synergistically, each talking past the other, each accusing the other of overlooking what is most fundamental about human nature.

My personal experience over more than three decades could be characterized as an attempt to foster a dialectic of mutual engagement and mutual influence between these two vantage points. The side of me trained as a psychoanalyst, the side that had learned how to seek out hidden trauma and vulnerability, needs to continually be reminded that, at the most essential level, nothing is missing—and nothing is hidden. Meanwhile, the side of me that delighted in the revelation of intrinsic wholeness needs ongoing reminders about the temptation to bypass the unresolved conflicts that lurk in the shadows cast by the light of realization.

We all face two challenges in accepting who we truly are. The first challenge is to accept our vulnerabilities and all those parts of our self about which we have grown up feeling ashamed and guilty, and about which we may be in denial. The second challenge is in facing the paradox of our perfection amid a life of suffering. Western psychotherapy has traditionally been focused on the first challenge, Buddhist practice on the second. While each has found ways of engaging with both sides of our nature, therapy typically runs the risk of seeing our flaws, symptoms, or deficits as central and its practice medicalized into an unending treatment of mental "illness." Buddhism foregrounds the realization of perfection, reaching down into that deep well of no-self, to a place beyond loss and gain. This approach, especially as it developed in twentieth-century America, runs the risk of emotional bypass, of imagining that deep-seated emotional problems and character pathology can be washed away solely by sufficiently deep realization without ever having to engage psychological problems directly.

It is my hope that in the discussion of koans that follow, the two sides may be brought together and that a psychologically minded approach to traditional Zen practice will emerge.

I will begin at the beginning, with what we know of the Buddha's life and the nature of the realization that he bequeathed to us.

The brief story of Shakyamuni Buddha's life in the *Transmission of the Lamp*—an account of the lives of Buddhist masters compiled in 1004 CE that became an *ur*-text for the later koan collections—is a mixture of parable and hagiography, from which it is difficult to glean more than a glimpse of the person who became known as the Buddha. The mythological quality of what passed for biography in those days is exemplified by the baby who proclaims immediately at birth, "In the heavens above, and in the four quarters of the earth, there is none holier than I."

However, the story of the infant Siddhartha also includes the early death of his mother. Although he is presented as growing up in a sheltered and privileged world, it would not be unreasonable for us to imagine this loss as fuel for his later questing. It is perhaps a measure of all historical, cultural, or hagiographic gaps that his mother's death is never given credit for spurring his latter quest to unravel the mystery of life and death, the way it does for the great eleventh-century Japanese Zen master Dogen. It is only when as a young man, having been given a sheltered life by his father, that upon suddenly being confronted with the sight of an old man, a sick man, and a corpse, the reality of suffering and death become real to the young prince. He leaves home, which includes leaving a wife and young son, to dedicate his life to the esoteric ascetic practices of his day in his search for meaning. This paradigmatic home-leaving fits the model of renunciation that was the hallmark of all spiritual practices of his day and that continues to be a template with which we today must come to terms.

It is hard for us today to know how to imagine the forms of practice Siddhartha is said to have mastered. The *Lamp* records, "For the first three years he practiced the samadhi (deep meditation) of non-action, but found it no good and gave it up. The next three years he studied . . . the samadhi of non-thinking, but this too was no good and he gave it up." I find it's useful to think of them as different modes of mastery over mind and body, attempts to completely stop or control thought on the one hand and on the other to fully master all bodily needs and sensation. The *Lamp* goes on: "Then he went to Gaya Mountain and spent the next six years practicing ascetic disciplines together with many heretics, wearing sackcloth and eating but a little rye each day." Whether this extreme asceticism describes actual practices engaged in at the time or is part of a myth of life-and-death commitment constructed to exhort latter-day monks is probably unknowable. But the model of pushing oneself to the brink of death in the name of practice is one that, for better or worse, has shaped what it has meant to seek enlightenment ever since.

There's not much in this part of the story that I can identify with or would care to emulate. Long ago I intuited that whatever is there to realize about life and death is something that is hidden in plain sight. We struggle to accept the truth that has been there right before our eyes all along. Before setting out on his journey of discovery, the young prince Siddhartha is said to have looked upon old age, sickness, and death for the first time and been shaken to his core, saying to himself that those things "must ultimately be rejected." And yet, after all those years of struggle, the essence of his realization was precisely that old age, sickness, and death are inescapable, that impermanence is the most fundamental thing, not only about our human lives, but about everything in the universe. The intensity of his practice was proportionate to his resistance to this basic fact, and the depth of his realization corresponded to the thoroughness of his ultimate acceptance of what had been so utterly unacceptable when he first set out.

In the *Lamp*'s version of the actual moment of his enlightenment, it simply states that "when the morning star arose, the Bodhisattva became a buddha." Other accounts have him proclaiming in that moment that he and all beings together attained buddhahood. This never struck me as the sort of thing I could imagine anyone spontaneously proclaiming. I was grateful therefore to come across a version of the story told by Shodo Harada in which Shakyamuni looks up at the morning star and simply says, "That's me." Maybe when you hear the phrase "that's me," you imagine the Buddha proclaiming his "oneness" (whatever you imagine that is) with the star and everything in the universe. I have a different reaction.

I imagine him sitting under the tree after all those years of struggling to master his mind and body, struggling to master the secret of life and death. Suddenly, he looks at the star, twinkling in the sky, and realizes the star hasn't struggled at all in order to be just what it is, to be perfect, just as it is. And he thought, I too am just what I am, I'm exactly like that star, manifesting my nature perfectly moment after moment. And everything in the world, like me, like the star, is fully, perfectly, expressing its own nature. Everything in this moment is a buddha, a perfectly realized being. What a shame not to realize it, what a shame to imagine that a star—or any being—needs to become something more than it already is. What the star already is, however, is not some Platonically pure or eternal essence of "star-ness," but ever-changing. Perfection and change aren't opposites; they turn out to be synonyms. Not only don't we have to change in order to become perfect, our perfection manifests moment after moment in change itself.

Paradoxically, the very depth and thoroughness of Shakyamuni's realization of buddha nature continuously expressing itself throughout all of creation, a realization of wholeness that we all participate in, whether knowingly or unknowingly, creates a new gulf of separation. We are so in awe of the Buddha and the Buddha's enlightenment that we make him and it into something otherworldly, something transcendent and virtually unattainable. From "can't miss," we somehow go straight to "out of reach."

One day as a medical student studying psychiatry, I was sitting in a circle of patients and therapists engaged in group therapy. Suddenly, I was struck how every person in the room, patients and therapists alike, was perfectly expressing *who they were*, in every moment, down to the tiniest detail. How they dressed, their posture as they sat in their chair, how they tilted their heads, how they spoke or remained silent, every gesture, every intonation of their voice, absolutely nailed their character as if they were actors who had totally mastered their roles. It was astounding! How could they all have gotten themselves so exactly, so perfectly right?

But of course, how could they miss? Who, what else could they be or do other than exactly what they were doing? This was one of my first tastes of a "perfection" without content, of a "rightness" that wasn't achieved or approximated, but totally and always right there before my eyes, no matter which way I turned.

It was also a revelation that nothing is hidden. Everyone was fully displaying who they were. There was nothing more "behind the scenes" to uncover or decipher, the way my usual psychoanalytic mindset would lead me to think. There was both clarity and acceptance of each person being just who he or she was. Remarkably, the whole distinction between who was a patient and who was a therapist was forgotten, or perhaps was reduced to a nonqualitative, nonhierarchical difference—like who was wearing green and who was wearing blue.

I am not presuming to equate this minor personal insight with the Buddha's enlightenment. For one thing, such moments quickly pass, and our habitual sense of something being missing, something being wrong, quickly reasserts itself. But such moments give us a glimpse of another way of seeing ourselves, one which may spur us to further practice. We imagine the Buddha's enlightenment to have been total and thoroughgoing, with no problematic aspects of his earlier character unresolved, no attachments or delusions left undissolved, no questions left unanswered. For the rest of us, realization is never once and for all, and old doubts and old habits will resurface to be dealt with over and over throughout our life.

Yet doubt and old habits are part of how we twinkle like that star. As is sickness, old age, and death. And delusion and joy—the full spectrum of life as it is.

The koans that follow can all help us see who we really are, especially those parts of ourselves that we have, sadly, for one personal reason or another, tried to turn away from. We have all blinded our self to parts of life we reflexively have felt too painful to behold or face directly.

Like Shakyamuni, we must be able look up and say, "That's me."

CHAPTER TWO

WHO, ME?

MU

A monk asked Chao-chou (Jap. Joshu), "Does a dog have buddha nature or not?" Chao-chou answered "Mu."

In Zen lore, Shakyamuni's great enlightenment is said to have been realized in turn by his Dharma heir Mahakashyapa, who in turn passed it on to Ananda, and so on down to our present day. While the tradition of an unbroken one-to-one transmission cannot be shown to be historically accurate, in Zen we believe that Shakyamuni's original revelation is indeed available to each of us. The stories of insight and transmission collected in the classic koan collections are both testimony to this possibility and a toolkit for reproducing in our own lives the experiences they describe. For generations of Zen students, the koan Mu has been the first and often most powerful of these tools.

The practice of Mu is introduced to us in "Chao-chou's Dog," the first of forty-eight cases in the Wu-men kuan (Jap. Mumonkan), a thirteenth-century collection of koans. Robert Aitken translates "Wu-men kuan" as "The Gateless Barrier." Earlier translators have called it "The Gateless Gate." So much of our practice, and especially the practice of Mu, begins by correctly understanding that very title. What is it telling us?

When we first hear of a gateless barrier, we may imagine that it means an impenetrable barrier, one with no opening in the gate anywhere. Master Wu-men, the compiler of the Wu-men collection, calls it "the barrier of ancestral teachers" and challenges us to pass through. It is as if the old teachers set up this barrier to their elite club of realization and no one who doesn't know the secret password is allowed to enter. Over and over the teacher challenges us, "What is Mu?" We try every spell we can think of, from Abracadabra to Zen, but nothing works, every answer is rejected. As long as we are convinced that the gate is locked, we can never open it.

But actually the gatelessness of Mu means just the opposite of impenetrable: the gate, and life itself, is wide open to us just as it is—in fact, there is really no barrier anywhere. So why is there a problem? Why is Mu so difficult to pass through? Simply because we don't experience that openness in our lives at all. We feel that there are barriers everywhere, inside and out—barriers that we don't want to face or cross, barriers of fear, anger, pain, old age, and death. We think that all these forms of suffering block our path. We don't see or trust that they themselves are gates. Everything is a gate and we can enter anywhere.

The hard work of our practice is learning to recognize and acknowledge that we ourselves have imagined and set up these barriers. Only when we are really willing to enter the territory they have shut off from us will we find ourselves in that wide-open, barrierless life that Wu-men offered to show us.

At the most basic level then, this old story about Chao-chou, a monk, and a dog is all about the problem of separation, about the artificial barriers we experience within ourselves and between one another, cutting us off from life as it is. And Wu-men offers us the technique of concentrating on this one word, "Mu," as a way of breaking down these barriers. By becoming completely absorbed in Mu, the student, then as now, will first bump up against his own barriers, and then, by filling his whole consciousness with Mu, his whole world with Mu, the barriers will disappear, along with everything else, into this one word. Wu-men summarizes these different kinds of barriers with the simple phrase "has and has not," making this the paradigm of our dualistic thoughts and concepts. When Wu-men speaks of "great doubt," at one level we can feel the overwhelming confusion and perplexity of the monk trying to reach an intellectual understanding of Chao-chou's truly incomprehensible answer. Why does Chao-chou answer "Mu," which means "no," when every novice Buddhist knows that the answer should be "yes," that every sentient being has buddha nature?

The paradox of Chao-chou's answer arises out of a conflict between what the monk knows intellectually to be the right answer and his own deeply ingrained feeling that there is an unbridgeable gap between the rarified, spiritual world of buddha nature, which seems to exist millions of miles away from the real world of dogs and miserable, ordinary monks like himself. The gap, seemingly so real, is nonetheless a creation of his own thoughts, his own preoccupation with "have and have not."

Today we are more prepared to see the emotional underpinnings of our barriers. Wu-men's "red-hot iron ball" that we can neither swallow or spit up is a picture of how it feels to come to grips with that painful sense of separation we don't know how to escape. We practice by focusing on our own inner barriers, one by one, especially the emotional barriers of fear, pain, emptiness, and anger that manifest as hard knots of bodily tension. These are truly red-hot iron balls. These are feelings we've tried to stay separate from, and to keep them at bay we have erected barriers between ourselves and life. Moment after moment in the zendo, these barriers take the form of "This isn't it": *This moment is not what I want, what I'm trying to achieve or become. Not only is* this *not it, I am not it; I am not who I want to be.*

We are so alienated from our own wholeness that we can't begin to believe I am the answer to my own question. When I first got my medical degree and showed up at the hospital where I was to begin my residency training, for a long time I couldn't get used to being called "Dr. Magid." Who, *me*?

Mu is emotional flypaper. All our issues begin to buzz around it and eventually get stuck to it. I know a strand of sticky flypaper covered with dead or half-alive struggling flies is a less grand image than a red-hot iron ball stuck in your gullet. But there's something to be said for taking the drama out of our struggles, seeing them more as pathetic and mundane rather than epic. One of those flies is the macho fly—a swaggering, noisy horsefly that is tougher than anybody, ready to endure anything, impervious to pain, and eager for any challenge, the harder the better. The traditional language of struggling with Mu always brings this fly out. Then there's a fragile little mayfly, weak and afraid, "I can't do it," or "I'll never be good enough." Maybe there's a certain benefit that comes from transforming weak mayflies into swaggering horseflies, but they both end up on the flypaper.

We are caught in the grip of our own unconscious beliefs—beliefs that have arisen as our own curative fantasies about what can end our suffering: "If only I were free of . . . If only I could have. . . ." These beliefs may reside for years outside our conscious awareness, masquerading as common sense.

I have often said that psychoanalysis, paradoxically, is a process in which we come to distrust our deepest feelings—to question all that we are sure is at stake when we keep parts of ourselves and our life at bay. In analysis, and in Zen, we may have to get worse to get better: what is called a therapeutic regression may entail the patient allowing of warded-off feelings of vulnerability, dependency, and neediness to emerge. The façade of compliance and accommodation we show to the world may begin to crumble and we may feel increasingly naked and exposed. "Great doubt" is Wu-men's name for the process of deconstructing all these inner barriers. And while for a long time we may merely feel that Mu—and our failure to "answer" it—is progressively stripping away all that we know and have relied on in the past, paradoxically, it is in the midst of doubt and not knowing that our habitual ways of thinking and separating ourselves from the world lose their grip. We can truly become Mu only when we have finally ceased trying to understand it.

The Zen teacher demands that of the student, "What is Mu?"— this is precisely like asking, "What is life?"

You can't answer by somehow standing outside of life, examining it and offering your description. You yourself must become the answer.

Our practice, like our life, is both simple and difficult. The difficulties, as we know, are multiple and endless; Buddha included them all under the general rubric of "suffering." In therapy we can achieve a measure of comfort and relief by having someone explore and understand what we're going though in our suffering. We have a natural human desire to be understood, and feeling understood in itself gives us a kind of strength to face the difficulties life brings. We have an equally human desire to escape our suffering. Feeling understood also provides a supportive context within which we are able to face and experience the reality of suffering, rather than divert ourselves with one of our habitual tactics of denial or avoidance. While therapy may be good at exploring the difficulty in our lives, it traditionally has not provided a way to deeply experience the essential *simplicity* of our life.

Whether practicing Mu or just sitting, we settle into the simplicity of the moment, this moment's completeness and immediacy. This moment, just as it is, is all there is. This moment, just as it is, is exactly, perfectly, just what it is. This moment, just as it is, is not happening to me, or inside my mind; the whole world, of which I am an inseparable part, is what's happening, right here, right now. There is no place to stand outside this moment, outside of myself, outside of the world. This moment, this self, this world, all one thing, all Mu.

So often we imagine we need an explanation of why things are the way they are. We want to know why we suffer, why we grow old, why we die. We look at our practice and we may ask why do we sit, why do we bow? All these questions, at every level, are dissolved in the experience of Mu. We find there is nothing whatsoever behind our experience, explaining or justifying it.

Why are we alive? We are alive! Why do we suffer? We suffer. Why do we die? We die. It's like asking, why do fish swim? They're fish! Why does the bear shit in the woods? And why is the Pope Catholic?

Although the basic practice at our zendo is shikantaza, or "just sitting," I sometimes offer students the opportunity to sit with Mu. However, I don't treat it as a beginning koan or one I give indiscriminately to one and all. I don't treat it as a barrier to be broken through or passed. I want students to sit with Mu only when they are more practiced observers of their own process, whether through sitting or therapy practice. I want them to be able to experience all the emotional dualisms that Mu evokes and actively engage their conflicts and self-hate through the koan.

We practice with Mu in a way that Mu absorbs everything into itself. We use Mu to enter more deeply into our bodies and our feelings, not to push our feelings away. It's like breaking up with your boyfriend, and while feeling all that pain and heartbreak you break into a wailing heartfelt version of an old Patsy Cline song. The more you feel your loss, the more urgently you sing it, and the more the song contains and intensifies everything you're feeling. Any difference between you, your pain, and the song vanishes. So it is with Mu. All the pain and frustration and judgment become

Mu. Mu becomes everything, and at the same time Mu is just Mu. All our pain and emotion and thought are just pain, emotion, and thought. Each moment is just what it is. There is nothing to do and nowhere to go. No question and no answer. No barrier and nothing beyond the barrier.

We see for ourselves that the "no" of Mu isn't the opposite of "yes." It is the negation of distinction, the negation of opposites; Mu negates the difference between "has" and "has not." Mu denies there is any difference between "dog" and "buddha nature." By undercutting the instinctive tendency to frame our experience into likes and dislikes, into self and other, into the admirable and the shameful, what we want to be and what we are afraid we are, Mu dissolves all the boundaries, drawing everything into an undifferentiated immediacy.

Mu is a powerful practice that has indeed entangled the eyebrows of successive generations of Zen students. That power does not come without a price or without pitfalls. There is a very real danger that Mu itself can be used to avoid or bypass emotional reality rather than engage it directly. Used as a one-pointed focus of concentration, a student can spend years trying to push everything out of awareness except Mu. Rather than everything coming in and becoming part of Mu, Mu forces itself out into the world, pushing everything aside, filling everything with Mu. We should remember Dogen's words that "carrying the self forward to confirm the myriad dharmas is delusion; the myriad Dharma advancing to confirm the self is realization."

Mu is a powerful *samadhi* generator—a way to enter into a special state of consciousness that temporarily banishes the pain and confusion of daily life. It is indeed glorious to enter into a state that banishes pain—but like all painkillers it can become addictive. We can become proud of our effort and energy in entering samadhi. We relish the joy it brings, and more and more the point of practice becomes to return to this blissful oasis. Although Mu unlocks a world without separation and difference, the subjective experience of kensho, the moment of falling away of all separation, can be intoxicating or even dangerous. Because of the intensity of the experience itself, students almost inevitably take the experience of opening itself as an "experience" they've "had." Paradoxically, a moment's experience of nonseparation can become immediately incorporated into a person's system of distinctions, and the fuel for the ultimate dualism of delusion and enlightenment.

Suddenly we have a new model of how we want our mind to be, a new picture of freedom from all those aspects of ourselves we've been avoiding feeling. Even though the moment of realization may have come about precisely when all our efforts and hopes for attainment failed us and left us wide open and vulnerable, our ingrained systems of self-hate and self-improvement stand all too ready to incorporate this new experience into their compulsive quests.

We may become trapped in a new dualism of our own making, one that starkly contrasts the confusion we feel off the cushion with the empowerment we feel while sitting. Our initial attempts to bring that sense of empowerment off the cushion and into our lives, however, may risk becoming a function of our preexisting egotism. We may have begun to think of ourselves as a special sort of person, with a powerful and esoteric practice accessible only to a small elite. At last, we imagine we have entered into the select coterie of the ancient teachers. Arrogance and narcissism (in the form of a preoccupation with our own condition and attainment) are the all-too-common byproducts of a practice gone astray. Mu is a powerful medicine for the disease of self-centeredness, but as with all medicine it's good to be aware of the possible side-effects.

Our first experience of realization is likely to be radically antinomian—a "seeing through" to the emptiness of custom, rules, and social norms to a liberating sense of unconstrained, limitless possibility. That first step, though radically liberating in one sense, can prove radically alienating in another, if it cuts us off from a sense of belonging, of participating in all the positive aspects of tradition, kinship, and community. If we can belong anywhere (one sense of being "cosmopolitan"—a citizen of the universe), we don't truly belong to any one place either. Indeed when Diogenes the Cynic first declared himself to be a cosmopolitan it was a scandalous idea, not an expression of liberal fellow feeling with all mankind. It carried the connotation of having no allegiance to any one particular city-state, a condition of profound disconnection from one's family, kin, and place of origin. That liberation into a deracinated brand of freedom is what Alan Watts once called "Beat Zen." That's no place for our practice to stop, but like adolescence, it would be a shame not to go through it at least once.

We see a version of it in case 4 of the Blue Cliff Record:

> When Tê-shan arrived at Kuei Shan, he carried his bundle with him into the teaching hall, where he crossed from east to west and from west to east. He looked around and said, "There's nothing, no one." Then he went out.
>
> But when Tê-shan got to the monastery gate, he said, "Still I shouldn't be so coarse." So he reentered [the hall] with full ceremony to meet [Kuei Shan]. As Kuei Shan sat there, Tê-shan held up his sitting mat and said, "Teacher!" Kuei Shan reached for his whisk, whereupon Tê-shan shouted, shook out his sleeves, and left.

Since Tê-shan remembered his manners, and returned to formally pay his respects to the master, we won't consign him to the Beat Zen category once and for all. And Kuei Shan himself predicts that the young whippersnapper will one day grow into a mature master. But, in the moment, like the comment on the case says, he was "completely exposed." Free, yes, but also trapped in the unconventionality that is a hallmark of being intoxicated with emptiness.

There is an even more perniciousness side effect of misunderstanding the nature of *kensho*, of seeing through to one's self-nature. Seeming breakthroughs have offered justification for bypassing psychological conflict in the process of cultivating a narrowly focused wholeheartedness. The scandals and misconduct that rocked many Zen communities should be seen retrospectively as important data as to the nature and limitations of so-called enlightenment experiences. Too often I have heard students and teachers alike try to attribute the repeated problems to a variety of related causes: the teacher in question wasn't "really" enlightened or hadn't fully completed his or her training, or there was some irregularity that could be used to cast doubt on the legitimacy of his or her authorization. The implication is always that when the traditional system is rigorously followed, these sorts of problems would be weeded out. Yet anyone who knows the intimate history of Zen in America must know it has not been a handful of rogue self-appointed teachers who caused most of the problems. Rather, the misconduct has been committed by the most eminent, impeccably trained, and officially authorized masters.

One can only conclude that traditional Zen training has never in and of itself been an adequate treatment for emotional conflict, character pathology, or substance abuse. Too often we seem to want to have it both ways; no teacher claims Zen is a cure-all and at the same time many teachers will blithely proceed as if sufficient sitting or koan practice will eventually take care of everything, with psychotherapy prescribed only for those unable to handle the rigors of training. Many personal problems, many forms of suffering are clearly eliminated in the course of long practice, but many other sorts of problems are just as clearly liable to be split off, compartmentalized, or denied at every level of attainment.

The biography of Jun Po Denis Kelly describes an encounter he had with the Dalai Lama in which he and other teachers raised this issue of teacher misconduct. The Dalai Lama maintained that any teacher who engaged in that sort of behavior simply hadn't had a deep enough realization. "When the insight of your true nature is deep enough," he explained, "it transforms all parts of us, so that Basic Goodness and compassion naturally arise. This prevents the kind of deluded behavior we see in such cases." *"Bullshit,"* said Jun Po, citing one offending teacher's decades of training, including ten years with the Dalai Lama himself. How could anyone maintain the teacher hadn't had deep enough insight? "That is because your insight isn't deep enough," replied the Dalai Lama.

I'm inclined to say they both had a point. The Dalai Lama's statement is on one level obviously true; anyone acting from self-centered motives in sexually exploiting his students has not had a deep enough realization. But the diagnosis is a tautology; by definition that behavior can't coexist with complete realization. The problem is, as Jun Po pointed out, there is no reliable correlation between what looks like years of practice and attainment by every other available criteria (e.g., completion of koan study, authorization to teach, or any other such thing) and the transformation of character that would guarantee such misconduct would not occur. If a teacher with decades of practice and teaching experience, who has had what are, by all accounts—including his own teacher's—genuine experiences of kensho, has not had a "deep enough" realization for his students to feel safe, what does it say about the efficacy of the method of training? It also begs the question as to whether ethical behavior, the capacity to actually adhere to the precepts, shouldn't be reliably grounded in something more generally available than complete enlightenment.

If the level of realization the Dalai Lama is talking about is our criteria, it looks like we are dealing with the spiritual equivalent of the lottery, in which the big prize goes to only one person in many millions. Sure, lots of us will get some benefits as runners-up, but the "real" thing is so rare as to be virtually unattainable. We might even ask what role training has at all in producing someone like the Dalai Lama. Like musical training for Mozart, it may have been a necessary but not sufficient condition for his genius to unfold. But that kind of genius (or that depth of enlightenment) may not be something that anyone else could ever attain no matter how hard or long they practiced. No amount of practice will turn Salieri into Mozart, but it can help the Salieri in all of us accept being Salieri and not torment himself for not being Mozart.

We need to be able to judge our practice not on the basis of a few rare and extraordinary individuals but what it does and doesn't do—for run-of-the-mill students and teachers like ourselves. I'm betting that a synergistic integration of Buddhist practice with psychoanalytic psychotherapy will help raise the payoff for the rest of us.

CHAPTER THREE

THE UNCONSCIOUS

"WHO PUT YOU IN BONDAGE?"

Seng-ts'an (Jap. Sosan), the Third Patriarch, was asked by a fourteen-year-old novice monk, "Pray, Master, of your mercy, allow me to beg you for the teaching of emancipation." The master asked, "Who put you in bondage?" The young monk answered, "No one has bound me." The master asked, "Then why do you seek for further emancipation?"

We can find versions of this question in many places and in many traditions. It would not seem out of place in the writing of Epictetus or other Stoic philosophers. For the Stoics, freedom meant first and foremost learning to distinguish what is under our control and what is not. The outer world is governed by chance and forces out of our control that range from the purely physical (like illness and natural disaster) to other people and their judgments of us. Our inner life, the Stoics taught, was the domain of true freedom. Our thoughts and judgments, the capacity to assent or dissent to the truth of a proposition, was ours alone to make.

This young monk was remarkable in being awakened by these words and went on to become the Fourth Ancestor. But most of us, even though we know that no one other than ourselves has put us into bondage, are unable to untie the psychological knots that bind us so tightly. For most of us, some *other*, some inaccessible part of our self, has gotten us tied up. The tying of the knots has been the result of an *unconscious* process, one whose steps we cannot remember and whose results we cannot undo.

It is the work of psychoanalytic therapy to gradually uncover just how we feel ourselves to be constricted and in what relational and emotional context the bonds were forged. A typical narrative might involve our parents' anxiety in the face of their child's natural expressions of aggression, playfulness, or emergent sexuality. All too often, the parents pass along the message that the child's spontaneous, exuberant behavior is too much for the parent to bear and that parental love is contingent on the child's suppressing the full range of his or her own feelings. In order to maintain a secure attachment with their parents, children may learn not only not to show anger but not to *feel* anger, not only not to show vulnerability or neediness but not to allow themselves to even feel the need in the first place. Children's anger, their neediness, their spontaneity, may be split off, repressed, or dissociated, so that it no longer feels like a part of themselves. Sent underground, these emotions may fester and emerge in a new relational context as forbidden, perverse, addictive, or compulsive behaviors. Dependency and need for soothing, unacknowledged and delegitimized, may force itself back into our lives in the form of addictive behavior or masochistic and submissive relationships.

Like the law of the conservation of energy in physics, psychoanalysis posits the *law of inescapability*. As Jessica Benjamin describes it, "Something that is pushed out of one psychic space . . . has to go elsewhere . . . likewise what one refuses to recognize outside reemerges as a dangerously threatening internal object." We inevitability, it seems, strive after an unattainable unity, a nonconflicted sense of ourselves as good, idealistic, compassionate; or conversely attribute those idealized qualities to some Other, an enlightened buddha for instance, while keeping within ourselves a picture of our own self as tainted by delusion, desire, anger, and attachment. Having split off our own intrinsic wholeness and projected it into the image of an idealized enlightened Other, we carry the image of perfection within ourselves in the guise of aspiration but in reality allowing it to punitively remind us that we are forever falling short, forever hopelessly short of our goal. Alternately, we can project our limitations and ambivalence onto others: the spouse who does not practice meditation, an outside world preoccupied with material-ism, the beginner on the adjacent cushion who just can't sit still.

All these attempts at making intolerable attributes "not me" end up polluting our experience of others and the world. Trying to excrete what we are ashamed of in ourselves, we piss in our own relational pool and end up contaminated instead of purified.

Whatever we try to bury away deep within ourselves, out of guilt, shame, or fear, that very thing, just by virtue of now being deep within our psyche, will take on the guise of being our inner-most, secret self. Denial and repression thus take on qualities of self-fulfilling prophecies. Because I cannot bring myself to speak of what I am most ashamed, it becomes literally as well as metaphor-ically unspeakable. It becomes the "me" that nobody knows, and that *me*, I then fear, is the "real" me. In both therapy or meditation practice, we are torn between a desire to become once and for all transparent, to be seen and be known through and through, and an equally powerful countervailing fantasy of having the shameful, hidden me extirpated once and for all or driven into ever deeper recesses by the triumph of our idealized or enlightened self.

The solution must come from the other direction. As Jessica Benjamin explains, "Difference, hate, failure to love can be sur-mounted not because the self is unified, but because it can tolerate being divided." That tolerance means a re-owning of what has been excluded—re-owning both our perfection and our failures. Like *The Tempest*'s Prospero, facing Caliban, we must able to say: ". . . this thing of darkness I / Acknowledge mine."

How can koans address these unconscious processes? Unfortunately, most of the time, they simply don't, and the liberation we feel in one part of our lives leaves us in bondage in another. Yet, clearly, for some percentage of individuals, the koan unlocks the gate and we are able to move freely where previously we have felt fenced in. When the young novice Tao-hsin (Jap. Doshin) asked the Third Ancestor about emancipation, he was, in one sense, simply asking a stock question, as do so many of the monks who seem to serve as straight men to the masters in the koan stories. Yet for the master's answer to have the effect that it did, young Tao-hsin's personal sense of being in bondage must have been excruciatingly intense. He invested what might have been nothing more than a cliché with real, personal feeling. This is the challenge of koan practice: to make a thousand-year-old story the vehicle for concentrating and articulating our own present-day dilemmas. If our question—whether in our own words or in words we have learned by rote—genuinely digs down into our emotional core, an answer may be a true turning word, unlocking in a moment what had been imprisoned within us for a lifetime.

There remains the question of what exactly counts as "bondage," or its opposite, "emancipation." A fourteen-year-old novice monk in sixth-century China would be bound (as viewed through our contemporary standards) by a rigid set of material and cultural limitations that would circumscribe every aspect of his life. If we imagine substituting a fourteen-year-old girl for the novice in the story, the extent of the external constraints on her life would be even more obvious and dramatic.

Yet the bondage to which this monk refers is not social, cultural, or political but entirely internal and psychological. What is implicit in this view of "inner" bondage is a view of the mind that is constrained by its own desires, conceptions, and attachments that are arising spontaneously, so to speak, entirely from "inside" the person. Although we can speak in a Buddhist context of our conditioning and the dependent co-origination of all phenomena, our propensity to delusion and attachment is in some sense innate, part of what it means to be human.

We are not dealing here with a model of the mind in which the inner is constituted by a person's relations, in which our image of our self and others and our place in the world are internalized based on how we have grown up in a particular family, with particular parents and siblings, in an atmosphere either loving or neglectful, attentive or unresponsive to who we are and to our developmental needs. Ironically, somewhat like Freud with his *drive* theory, this Buddhist picture of the mind and its particular propensity to self-created bondage arises out of our innate biological/human nature. Our desires—whether for sex, attachment, control, or permanence—given the nature of reality (frustrating of our fantasies for Freud, impermanent and uncontrollable for Buddha) inevitably lead to what we complain about as suffering.

One can imagine at least part of what tormented the young novice. I don't think fourteen-year-olds have changed so much in a thousand years that sexual fantasies and masturbatory urges weren't part of his inner struggle and anguish. Masturbation provides adolescents with one of their first and clearest lessons in the two paths of self-control and self-acceptance.

Do they, and their parents and society, view their sexuality as something normal, to be enjoyed or as the prototypical bad habit, the first addictive behavior they must learn to master? Pure self-acceptance can easily become self-indulgence and it's the rare adolescent who will spontaneously choose homework over pornography if given unlimited freedom of choice. Yet the alternative path of self-control can mean being constantly at war with oneself. One may be winning this war, and one may feel proud of that fact—but life remains one of constant battle. Any adult who has ever tried to go on a diet has had the experience of this dilemma. Do you go down the path of eternal struggle and constant vigilance or the path of acceptance, of having that pie and ice cream and letting your weight just be what it is?

Zen practice can similarly oscillate between these two poles, one of ease and self-acceptance, the other of mastery and determination. Deep ditches lie on each side of the Middle Way.

In the traditional language of the Heart Sutra, we speak of suffering, as well as extinction and nirvana—words that imply ridding ourselves of something once and for all, a wiping away of the underlying causes of suffering leading to its extinction. The Heart Sutra tells us: "Avalokitesvara, Bodhisattva doing deep prajna paramita clearly saw the emptiness of all five conditions, thus relieving misfortune and pain." Yet if suffering arises seemingly inevitably out of our nature, how can it be eradicated? The traditional answer lies in what Buddha says is a basic confusion—or delusion—about our nature, indeed about the nature of everything in the world. Aspects of our nature that we (including Freud) take to be bedrock—things like desire and the objects of our desire—are in fact ephemeral. They all are subject to change and no desire can ever be truly fulfilled, no inner state can be permanent, no permanent sense of "me" can be maintained, protected, or held on to. One trap into which many practitioners fall is that having affirmed the emptiness or impermanence of all conditions, including inner ones, they then valorize "enlightenment" precisely as an unchanging, permanent inner state they hope one day to achieve.

The language of cessation or extinction flirts with evoking a new permanent state of affairs. Properly speaking, since the self—like everything else—is already empty (that is, impermanent)—cessation of self isn't something we have to achieve but something that, as the verse says, is already here.

When someone in our community is mortally ill, we add their name to the chant in our service, which prays, "May they be serene throughout their suffering. . . ." What does it mean to be serene in the midst of suffering? Is this the same as the relieving of misfortune and pain promised in the Heart Sutra? It seems to me that we would only be further deluding ourselves if we imagined attaining a state of consciousness via meditation that would transport us to a place where we literally felt no pain.

Though blissful states can suddenly emerge in the midst of physical pain during long periods of zazen, it does not seem to me to be the goal of our practice to enter such states once and for all and never feel pain again. That is the effect of a narcotic, not of insight and wisdom. No, somehow, our pain and serenity must coexist, neither obliterating the other. The Latin root of serenity, *serenus*, is an adjective that describes the weather, clear and cloudless, and by analogy our mood as cheerful, joyous, and tranquil. Our lives, and perhaps especially our inner lives, are very much like the weather, and sometimes we seem to have about as much control over one as the other.

Is it the goal of practice that life be a beach, a place of endless sun and a cloudless sky? No one is more upset than the person who has traveled hundreds (or thousands) of miles and spent hundreds (or thousands) of dollars to vacation on the beach, only to have it rain constantly throughout his or her vacation. How many meditators have I met who have spent hundreds (if not thousands) of hours on the cushion only to be dismayed that their mind is still subject to intrusive thoughts, their emotions still unruly, their bodies still grow old and painful in ways they just can't manage to control or be impervious to?

Serene in the midst of suffering, I've come to believe, can only mean *acceptance* in the face of suffering, the way I have had to accept wind and rain throughout my long anticipated beach vacation. I am neither an idiot nor a Pollyanna—I can tell sunshine from rain and I can't pretend I don't prefer one to the other any more than I can pretend I don't care whether the gout in my big toe goes away or not. Complete erasure of such difference is not in the cards—not in my cards anyway. But differences don't always have to make a difference. They don't have to lead to self-reproach, complaints about the unfairness of life, or prolonged futile attempts to control the uncontrollable.

It's somewhat ironic, and not a little sad, that many people who have practiced for decades are secretly ashamed at not having achieved some idealized state of equanimity, the image of which was planted in their imagination when they were beginners, and which has remained an unexamined aspect of what they call aspiration. This shame-inducing image of the transformations practice ought to have brought about after so many years has the quality of what Lauren Berlant has called "cruel optimism." Berlant defines this as a "desire [that] is actually an obstacle to your flourishing. It might involve food, or a kind of love; it might be a fantasy of a good life, or a political project . . . [or] a new habit that promises to induce in you an improved way of being."

I have written previously of the curative fantasies that all of us bring to the start of practice. These are inevitable and, like transference in a therapeutic relationship, are precisely what practice is designed to elicit and work through. Yet remnants of our old fantasies can remain lodged in our unconscious throughout a lifetime of practice and often reveal themselves when we find ourselves measuring ourselves against the descriptions of the enlightenment experiences of the old masters. But those old stories are themselves hagiographic constructions, arranged to one degree or another within a certain formulaic narrative structure, so as to illustrate and epitomize a traditional model of what constitutes a master and what constitutes the experience of enlightenment. At its most extreme, this can mean measuring ourselves against a fairy tale. Practice may, I hope, over time make me a somewhat wiser, less self-centered, more joyous person, but it will no more turn me into Shakyamuni (or Lin-chi or Dogen) than Gandalf.

Through practice, I can partake in something of those masters' insight and experience and make something of it my own, without having to indulge in the fantasy that I will literally experience what they experienced. Genius is by any definition rare, and religious genius is no exception. If, among the hundred or more Zen teachers who make up the American Zen Teachers Association, there is a modern-day master who has achieved the level of insight and artistic creativity of Hakuin, she has never revealed it while I was present.

Sometimes, as the saying goes, the perfect is the enemy of the good. We should not lament our lack of perfection—after all, I am capable of being perfectly myself—but rather use practice to explore why we feel inadequate if we are anything less than perfect by some abstract or idealized standard.

Joko Beck used to lament that students would turn even their experience of dying (or their expectations of what dying should be like for a Zen student) into something they could do well or badly. The fantasy of a "good death" reflects this picture of inner peace or serenity imperturbable by the vicissitudes of pain and illness. Didn't the old masters calmly announce their death days in advance to their disciples (even death couldn't take them by surprise!), and when the time came, write a perfect death poem only moments before expiring while seated in a full-lotus? Joko's own old age and death offered a profound lesson to her students but one that was not quite so neat and clean. She did live "serenely" well into her nineties and by all accounts passed from this life calmly after a long, slow fading away of her physical strength. But her personality underwent subtle changes in the years prior to her death, changes that no one quite knew how to understand or explain. She became estranged from two of her closest and most loyal Dharma heirs and attempted to revoke the transmission she had given them.

Had they changed or had she? To my mind, encroaching old age, physical frailty, and dependency, along with subtle neurological deterioration, took their toll on who she was and how she perceived what was happening around her. Can even Zen masters be subject, unknowing and unselfaware, to such fundamental changes in how they see themselves and others? We'd perhaps rather not think so, but the alternative in this case was to assume that *two* other Zen teachers had gone from being loyal and devoted disciples to selfish and scheming usurpers. Not a pretty picture whichever version you choose.

In the end, what we may need to be most free of, what keeps us most in bondage, is the very fantasy of absolute freedom itself.

CHAPTER FOUR

MOTIVATION TO PRACTICE

HAKUIN AND THE SOUND OF ONE HAND

Koan narratives rarely give us more than a glimpse of the inner turmoil that motivates the questioner. A rare exception is the case of Hakuin Ekaku (1686–1768), who has left us a unique document, a spiritual autobiography entitled *Wild Ivy*, that recounts how his youthful fears of hell were the spur to his practice. Although we don't usually think of Buddhism as a religion of fire and brimstone, as a young boy of eleven, Hakuin was taken to hear a sermon by a visiting Nichiren Buddhist preacher who described "in graphic detail the torments in each of the eight Scorching Hells. . . . He had every knee in the audience quaking, every liver in the house frozen stiff with fear. As little as I was, I was certainly no exception. My whole body shook with mortal terror. When I went to bed that night, even in the security of my mother's bosom, my mind was in a terrible turmoil. I lay awake sobbing miserably all night, my eyes swollen with tears."

After this, the boy developed a phobia of taking baths, the fire and boiling water having become traumatically associated with his image of hell. His mother, unable to comfort him in any other way, simply told him he must worship the deity of the local shrine and pray for deliverance. As a result he began getting up in the middle of the night, lighting incense, and praying for hours on end. He records his father's response to all this as less than supportive, "You little idler. Up every night, wasting good lamp oil. A little fellow like you, reciting sutras. What good will it do you?" We don't know just why young Hakuin was so preoccupied with his own sinful nature and the prospect of eternal damnation, but this picture of his father's harsh critical nature at least provides a clue.

Hakuin was ordained at the age of fourteen and entered formal Zen training with the explicit goal of relieving his own anxieties about damnation. He hoped that Zen would provide a release from torment. As a young monk, he idealized what he knew of the old Chinese masters. One day, however, he heard the story of the great master Yen-t'ou (Jap. Ganto) who gave a great shout as he was murdered by a band of bandits. Hakuin was thrust back into despair—if a master like Yen-t'ou could not escape a painful death, what hope did he have? Hakuin practiced with great intensity trying to find the answer to his problem.

His autobiography is filled with accounts of the determination and austerity with which he practiced—going to such extremes as sitting on a plank suspended over a well—if he fell asleep he'd fall in and drown. Eventually, his practice culminated in a series of what he thought were experience of great realization, great *satori*. What is remarkable in Hakuin's record is the honesty with which he recounts how he nonetheless kept falling back into confusion or despair. After his first breakthrough, he felt that his body and mind had completely dropped away. "Overwhelmed with joy, I hollered at the top of my lungs, 'Old Yen-t'ou is alive and well!'" It sounds like a classic case that ends with the monk becoming enlightened, but what happened after that? Hakuin admits, "I became extremely proud and arrogant. Everyone I encountered seemed to me like so many lumps of dirt." Fortunately, he soon encountered a new teacher to whom he tried to display his enlightenment. "How do you understand the koan about the dog and the buddha nature?" the master asked him. Hakuin confidently shot back, "No way to lay a hand or foot on that." Whereupon the master grabbed him by the nose and said, "Got a pretty good hand on it there!"

Shoju Rojin, the master, admonished Hakuin that he must go forward with "continuous and unremitting devotion to hidden practice, scrupulous application." When Hakuin asked what this meant, Shoju retorted, "It certainly doesn't mean sneaking off to some mountain and sitting like a block of wood on a rock or under a tree 'silently illuminating' yourself. It means immersing yourself totally in your practice at all times and in your daily activities— walking, standing, sitting, or lying down. . . . Practice concentrated in activity is a hundred, a thousand, even a million times superior to practice done in a state of inactivity."

Hakuin recounts passing through all sorts of great satoris and great relapses into despair for another twenty years or so before finally curing himself of his various Zen sicknesses. Looking back, it became obvious how preoccupied with his own mind, his own subjectivity, he was during all those early years of practice.

Post-*satori* practice for Hakuin meant finally ceasing to be preoccupied with his own personal condition and attainment and to devote himself and his practice to helping and teaching others. Finally, at long last, he realized that true enlightenment is a matter of endless practice and compassionate functioning, not something that occurs once and for all in one great moment on the cushion.

Years later, Hakuin asked his disciple Torei Enji why he came to practice; Torei responded, "for the sake of all beings." Hakuin chuckled and replied that was better reason than his own. Personally, though, when I hear students say they are practicing for the sake of others, I am immediately suspicious. One is inevitably self-centered when one begins to practice. This is not a beginner's flaw; it's the very problem that practice is designed to address, even if it must do so indirectly. Rather than conceal our true motivation behind a veil of high-minded aspiration, we should use practice to honestly explore what has brought us to practice in the first place. As I have discussed elsewhere, we inevitably will discover that we all have a "secret practice," a personal psychological agenda and fantasy about how practice will relieve our suffering by eliminating those parts of ourselves that are the root of our problems or by actualizing some superhuman ideal.

Shohaku Okumura has described his own early years in a way that gives an example of a subtle form of secret practice. After graduation from college, he practiced with Kosho Uchiyama at Antaiji for five years. The practice there was pure and austere, focused on just sitting. "We sat nine (fifty minute) periods daily for more than a year. . . . During sesshin we sat fourteen periods a day for five days. We had no ceremony, no chanting and no lecture. We just sat." After Uchiyama's retirement in 1975, Okamura came to the United States with two other monks from Antaiji to establish a center in Massachusetts. In addition to attempting to maintain their rigorous practice, the monks, having no financial support from Japan, had to do a great deal of manual labor to support themselves; digging a well by hand, cutting enormous quantities of firewood, working for local farmers and even in a local tofu factory. The result of all this physical labor: "After five years, I had pain in my neck, shoulders, elbows and knees. . . . I couldn't work and sitting sesshin was very difficult. . . . I had to return to Japan." Unable to practice because of his health, he was at a loss. He realized that, although Uchiyama had always stressed (and he thought he had known) that one should not practice zazen for gain, he had unconsciously been doing just that. "I wanted to live a better life than ordinary people," he concluded.

He had fallen into the arrogance of elitism and identified practice with a way of life available only to the young and healthy. Only when he was physically unable to practice the way he thought he "should" was he able to gradually find his way toward truly just sitting, with no hope or expectation of anything beyond sitting itself. It is unfortunately the case that sometimes we can only come to see our secret practice involuntarily, when something in our life makes it impossible to hold on to. Only then do we see what we've really been doing. But Okamura's story also reveals the way that a seemingly clear and rigorous practice, even one ostensibly centered on "just sitting," can hide a personal agenda. Sitting itself may not be enough to reveal our secret practice; that's where I hope that a psychologically minded teacher can make a difference.

Hakuin's story, on the other hand, exemplifies how personal fears can make for an entirely conscious goal-oriented practice. As they should, since our practice is premised on the Buddha's promise that there is both a cause and an end to suffering. Yet his story also shows how our practice can be diverted into a pursuit of super-humanness out of a desire to be impervious to what no one can be impervious to. We imagine that only by transcending what it is to be human will we be able to endure being human. Hakuin, like many masters before him, put himself through incredibly austere, ascetic, and self-punishing practices. We are sometimes told that the depth of masters' enlightenment is directly proportional to the severity and austerity of their practice.

I don't believe it. (Of course, you may rejoin that I'm no Hakuin, so how should I know?) I suspect instead that the intensity of Hakuin's practice reflects his desperate psychological condition and that in some sense the solution he chose mirrored the very problem he was trying to solve. He tortured himself in this life to escape his fears of being tortured in the next. Perhaps sometimes we have no choice. We must reenact the very thing we fear in order to come to terms with it.

We should be very cautious about drawing a means-to-an-end

lesson from this. The release we feel from taking off tight shoes may be proportional to how tight they were in the first place, but that doesn't mean that our practice should be putting on extra-tight shoes so we can have all the greater relief when we take them off. As a teacher, over the years, I have seen many, many different varieties of kensho experienced by my students, and there has never been any simple direct correlation between the intensity or length of their practice and the depth of their realization.

Many students, and not a few teachers I have known, have had what can only be described as a spontaneous kensho—an opening that came seemingly out of nowhere in their everyday life. Rather than being the result of long years of practice, that initial opening brought them to practice in an attempt to understand and deepen whatever it was that had happened to them. For every Hakuin, there may be a Hui-neng who was awakened the first time he heard a verse from the Diamond Sutra being recited.

Zen is in need of the idea of *grace*, the recognition that insights do not always come about as the result of our efforts but may arrive gratuitously, as gifts that we have done nothing to earn or deserve. There is a tendency in some Zen circles to an attitude that I can only describe as harshly moralistic and arrogantly elitist. Realization comes only to those who earn it by austerity, intensity, and superhuman effort and endurance. God (or Buddha) does not reveal himself to wimps.

Hakuin denounced his near-contemporary Bankei (1622–1693) for suggesting that the unborn, our true nature, was available to anyone, anywhere, anytime. Bankei's Zen was democratic rather than elitist, popular rather than esoteric. However, Bankei's lineage did not survive, and the heirs of Hakuin are sure they know the reason. But history is written by the victors and we should be careful of what lessons we draw. After all, Chao-chou's lineage died out as well. It is perhaps an all-too-human tendency among teachers to assume that whatever austerities they went through on the way to their own realization were the necessary conditions for that realization to occur and that their students' path should follow their own. But the path of realization is anything but linear. Zazen, as Dogen tells us, is not a means to an end.

Our path will start with whatever curative fantasies we harbor and it will meander through many byways of trial and error as we slowly, reluctantly come to face life as it is.

Like Hakuin, we must first confront the fears we come to practice to evade and then confront the egotism and sense of specialness unleashed by our initial experience of having seemingly transcended what we most feared.

We must confront our preoccupation with our own level of attainment, our tendency to use *dokusan*, meetings with a Zen teacher, as one more opportunity to "see what condition my condition is in." We must confront the temptation to use practice to make us in some way special and different from others, rather than as a tool to not just break down barriers between self and other but to enable us to reach out to the other in a meaningful and compassionate way. It is only in that reaching out that what had been our "personal" practice can truly go beyond the personal.

Hakuin devised the koan "What Is the Sound of One Hand?" as a challenge to our practice at every one of these levels. Although it can be used as a first koan in the manner of Mu, we can also use it to illuminate practice at many levels beyond an initial breakthrough.

First of all, what does "one" hand imply? Obviously, we usually clap with two hands—let's take that as a metaphor for our usual dualistic way of thinking. "*One* hand" therefore asks us to put aside duality and manifest oneness. How do you do that? What is an expression of reality before we divide it up into subject and object? A koan asks us to manifest oneness by becoming one with the koan itself. What is Mu? Totally become Mu. To become one with one hand, we do what? There's a wonderful scroll by the early twentieth-century master Nantembo where he's inked his right hand and impressed a handprint right onto the scroll.

To be one with the *sound* of one hand is to be one with what? What sound expresses undifferentiated reality? Silence is one kind of genuine presentation, when it is the silence of being fully present, yet fully emptied of self; body and mind having dropped away into a bottomless silence. This is a silence that manifests itself only after years of practice. Don't confuse it with the silence of simply not knowing how to answer. *WHAT!* is another presentation—in the midst of a shout we can't help but be fully present, there's no place for a thought or judgment to intrude. Lin-chi and a lot of old teachers liked that kind of presentation: the shout or the slap that obliterated any thought, any duality. What is Buddha? "Come closer and I'll tell you." *WHACK!* When Lin-chi first asked his teacher Huang-po that question, he got hit—only later did he realize he wasn't being punished—he had been given the answer. Of course, such behavior can quickly become stereotyped and over the years became a caricature of "Zen" behavior. How can you make it new? Sometimes our "self" disappears in the very action of answering a koan; sometimes we can only answer by being fully, totally, idiosyncratically our selves. Then who knows what will be revealed?

I just came across a scroll by a eighteenth-century master named Daikuku Seppou (d.1761), nicknamed Datsue-Seppou, who apparently was known for taking his clothes off in public (the Nudist Buddhist?). Now, there's a presentation of Naked Reality for you.

The Soto tradition has cultivated a different expression of non-separation, the kind manifested in the wholehearted attention to the details and rituals of everyday life. It has more in common with the subtle Zen of Master Chao-chou, who quietly offers newcomers and old hands alike a cup of tea. We should recall that Chao-chou didn't shout "Mu" at the monk who asked about the dog and buddha nature. In fact, in another version of the story, two different monks ask him the same question and he answers "no" to one and "yes" to the other. This is the Zen of "being just this moment." Nothing special, nothing even to call "Zen." All of these are ways we can express "oneness." Funny, in a way, isn't it, that there are so many?

So far, we're treating "the sound of one hand" as a koan like Mu, and indeed Hakuin used the koan as an initial concentration device to push beginning students to have that first experience of oneness. Actually, you can't "answer" Mu or any initial koan—the only "answer" is to have a certain kind of experience. Then you just show yourself—but your "self" is no longer in the picture the way it was before. But Hakuin doesn't stop there. The next level this koan addresses has to do more specifically with another sense of the word "sound." Having achieved oneness, what is its sound? In other words, how does it reverberate? How does it go out into the world and function? If we're just being "one" with our own hand, what have we accomplished? If it's all about our own private experience, it's nothing but a handjob. (Sorry, folks, I just couldn't resist that . . .)

The hand of oneness has to reach out and become the hand of compassion. An extended hand, not a silent, impassive hand. Further, once the right hand realizes it is part of one body along with the left hand, the two function together as one. Then clapping itself can be an expression of the functioning of the one hand. Our two hands do not function separately, but each acts as part of one body, making one sound. "Oneness" no longer is something we achieve as the result of our practice, some special state we enter into through sitting, but rather is the way things already are in their natural state of interconnectedness. Hakuin himself finally came to understand that after all his impressive satoris, if they amounted to nothing more than cultivating his own private experience, he would end up being what Hakuin calls "no different from a sleepy-happy old polecat drowsing away down inside his comfortable den." Teaching became the vehicle for Hakuin to finally get outside of himself, to travel, to lecture, to go wherever he was asked on behalf of others. All of us have to find our own realization, and our own expression, our own sound, our own voice.

The question of why we practice evolves out of our initial desire to attain some goal, out of our personal "secret practice" of escaping some part of ourselves or some part of life as it is, into a desire to fully and compassionately express who we are. We must make our own sound in the world, a sound that goes forth from our realization, a sound that reverberates out across the gap of separation.

CHAPTER FIVE

TRADITION & THE THIRD

HUANG-PO AND GOBBLERS OF DREGS

Huang-po (Jap. Obaku), instructing the community, said, "All of you people are gobblers of dregs. If you go on traveling around this way where will you have today? Do you know that there are no teachers of Zen (Chan) in all of China?"

At that time a monastic came forward and said, "Then what about those in various places who order followers and lead communities?"

Huang-po said, "I do not say that there is no Zen, it's just that there are no teachers."

Joko Beck, in her own version of this koan, likened students to baby birds, craning their necks, mouths agape, waiting for her as their teacher to drop some predigested morsel down their desperately eager throats. Whether it's grubs or dregs, the issue is the same: what can we ever expect to be given by someone else, especially someone else we've designated a teacher, someone who has what we lack? Joko used to insist that life is the only teacher and to make sure we didn't forget the point she enshrined the line "each moment, life as it is, the only teacher" into the Four Practice Principles (her modern version of the Four Noble Truths) that were recited at the end of every day's sitting. Huang-po, in his way, says there is only Zen, no teachers. In the context of the koan, we are meant to see that there can be no teacher or teaching outside our own experience. Don't set up a "teacher" outside of yourself. The teaching doesn't come from the outside, it is freely available to each of us if we only know how and where to look.

Yet, there is, in fact, much that comes from the outside, that as Zen students we partake of and are grateful for. We can sum up that kind of teaching with the word *tradition*. Is tradition the same as "dregs"? Is tradition only secondhand, predigested pablum, a poor substitute for having our own realization?

On one hand, it's absolutely true that we can't put anyone else's head on top of our own, but on the other it's equally true that we can see as far as we do because we are standing on the shoulders of the giants who've come before us. The Dhammapada, the Heart Sutra, the Platform Sutra, the Wu-men kuan, and the Blue Cliff Record: all dregs, all stories about other lives, other peoples' realizations. But if they are dregs, they are also enormously nourishing and satisfying dregs, dregs that fuel and inspire our practice and offer a rich vocabulary from which to fashion the Dharma in our own day.

We each have to have an experience that is genuinely our own, but we do not have to reinvent the wheel. We do not each have to invent zazen for ourselves; it is there for us to find and learn how to make our own. I used to liken *sesshin*, intensive meditation retreats, to an escalator: our task is to just take that first step, and let it carry us where we would not know how to go on our own. In our zendo, we alternate chanting the Heart Sutra and certain other verses in English and Sino-Japanese, a reminder that Ordinary Mind was not invented in Southern California. Our practice is a dialectic between self-discovery—what no one can do for us—and self-forgetting—a forsaking of will and a surrender into a life and practice that is not of our creation.

What we surrender to likewise has a double aspect: there is the Absolute within every moment, a space we experience as timeless and beyond conditioning, and there is the relative moment—a particular historical moment. Indeed, the practice and tradition we depend and build upon exists because of the efforts of particular individuals, operating within a particular culture and whose expressions of realization are inevitably shaped and colored by their time and circumstance. We are inspired by and uphold an idea of the Dharma that exists beyond space and time, yet we know of it only through the lives, efforts, and words of historical beings. Like Justice, the Dharma may be a timeless ideal, yet like justice, it will not mean the same thing in India as China as Japan as America, the same as it was two thousand years ago as it is today.

In relational analysis, "the Third" (or *thirdness*) refers to our co-creation and the mutual maintaining of a practice or perspective, whether within the dyad of the analysis itself or within the larger context of the whole field. *Thirdness* is defined in contrast to *complementarity* (another word for "dualism"), a state where my point of view is in opposition to your point of view. In complementarity, one of us of is right and one is wrong; one of our views will prevail over the other. In thirdness, however, what is true must be mutually arrived at and negotiated. The Third does not represent the compromise solution we ultimately arrive at or any set of rules for getting there. Rather it represents the whole state of mind that makes truly engaging with an other possible. For this to happen, we must be capable of recognizing the perspective of the other as representing a genuinely different and genuinely legitimate way of organizing his or her experience. This interplay of mutually recognizing subjects is called "intersubjectivity."

The capacity for thirdness thus requires that each party be capable of what Kohut called *empathy*, the capacity to see the world through the eyes of another and to see it as subjectively true as our own way of seeing—without presuming there is necessarily any outside, neutral, or objective place to stand from which to judge the correctness of one view over another. This psychoanalytic technical sense of empathy thus extends far beyond our ordinary use of the word to refer to being able to feel what another is feeling. Empathy, for Kohut, stands in contrast to objective, scientific *knowing*, where the assumption is that there are such things as experimentally verifiable "facts."

Within the realm of intersubjectivity—which includes what we refer to as the psychological, ethical, artistic, religious, and so forth, there is no such outside place to stand. This realm, we might say, is constituted by and within human relations. Water and rocks and the sun might all exist in a universe without people, but art, money, and marriage are things that only exist within the realm of language and human relating. What counts as "fair," just as what counts as "beautiful," is not something we can objectively discover or determine; both individually and culturally they must be negotiated and mutually agreed upon. Both empathy and thirdness require a degree of *surrender* of the self, a letting go of the primacy of one's own point of view and the *recognition* of the separateness and difference of other minds.

We can think of a tradition as both the record and holder of that mutual endeavor. A tradition embodies the working out of a form of life, practice, or perspective that may be in part, but never wholly, of my own creation. To partake of a tradition, we must be prepared to surrender to it to some significant degree; that is, we must be prepared to let go of our own personal point of view and allow ourselves to be immersed in this larger Third, the holder of the points of view of all those who have gone before me. At the most basic level of daily practice, we participate in *ritual*, literally entering into the forms and actions of our ancestors. Ritual is an opportunity to surrender our individual likes and dislikes, our personal opinions about how and why something is done. At the symbolic and psychological level, surrender stands in for the traditional monastic practice of home leaving. We leave the presumed safety of our self-centeredness and surrender our own point of view to that of the tradition, and to the Dharma.

When Huang-po says there is Zen but no teachers of Zen, a contemporary psychoanalyst might hear him as saying that there is only the Third of Zen to which we must all surrender. Don't get caught in the complementarity of "teacher" and "student," of "one has it, the other doesn't." There is just the Dharma, which is immediately available to you here and now.

But if we're not careful, this way of speaking can lead us down a metaphysical blind alley.

Is Zen, or the Dharma or buddha nature, some entity in its own right that timelessly exists apart from the lives of Zen teachers, apart from our own life, apart from life itself? What does it imply to say there is a teaching but no teacher?

Is the Dharma some pure, gem-like flame that is transmitted from generation to generation irrespective of the nature or quality of the human candle that carries it? Does it, unlike everything else, have some unchanging essential nature that exists apart from and is unsullied by its transitory human manifestation? Or do we understand the Dharma as an ongoing body of teaching and tradition in relation to the realization that no thing—including no teaching—can stand outside the realm of impermanence and cause and effect?

In all cultures, we find art, music, and religion. All cultures have a conception of the good, the true, and the beautiful. Yet there is no essential element common to art, music, and religion across all cultures. There is no single definition of the good, the true, or the beautiful that has applied throughout history. Poetry, for instance, comes down to us in the West from the time of Homer and Sappho. We can recognize what they have written as poetry even though the poetry of many modern poets would not be recognizable as poetry to them. The same is true of Western art and music. Abstract art would have been considered a contradiction in terms in cultures where art was synonymous with the mimetic, imitation of nature.

Art, music, poetry, and I suggest religion, including the Buddha Dharma, are "transmitted" generation to generation, the way all culturally defined activities are, embodied in the practices of the makers and the participants. Art, ultimately, is simply what the artists of a certain time and place create. Artists, musicians, priests, and teachers all occupy their respective cultural niches and the products of their activity are inseparable from the lives they lead in the making of it. There is no Platonic essence of Art that one generation of artists transmits to the next. Artists learn from, imitate, challenge, and subvert the art of their contemporaries and predecessors. All these interactions are what together constitute the mutually co-constructed thirdness of Art.

The idea of "Art" itself may be vital to each generation of artists, yet each generation will define and interpret the meaning of Art differently. If we try to find the essence of "Art," something that is true across all cultures and throughout time, we will be stymied. Yet Art continues to exist and flourish despite our inability to pin down its true nature. (It is an example of the sort of thing that functions well enough in practice, but will never work in theory . . .)The same holds true for our ideals of Justice, Love, and the Dharma. Perhaps what we want from Art and Love and Justice and the Dharma is for them to be timeless, pure, ahistorical. Thinking of them in that way may indeed help us hold on to them as ideals. Yet we know nothing is timeless, nothing undefined by the conditions of its arising.

Dharma teachers, like artists, learn from, imitate, challenge, and subvert the teaching of their teachers (think of Yasutani's relationship to his first teacher Nishiari and then to this later teacher Harada). The nature, the meaning of, the Dharma in any generation is nothing but the teaching, the behavior, the lives of those who are teaching and living it at any given time. The Buddhism of America both is and is not the Buddhism of Shakyamuni, and of our Chinese and Japanese ancestors. To turn Huang-po on his head: there is no Zen, only Zen teachers.

The Buddha Dharma is transmitted by and within the form of life of those who realize and practice it. Originally, this was a monastic lifestyle, a model that essentially claimed to be the sole manifestation of a true life of nonattachment. When we look at how the Dharma has been transmitted in America, we see that the forms of life involved have changed in many important ways. Japanese Zen underwent a radical change when at the end of the nineteenth century the Meiji government decreed that priests should marry and temples began to be passed down from father to son. Now in America, we have many forms of Buddhist practice coexisting, including the attempt to integrate Zen practice with lay life, which eliminates what was once the defining characteristic of the monastic: home-leaving. Yet despite these sea changes, we hold on to a vision of a single Dharma, preserved and transmitted from generation to generation. How much can the Dharma adapt to changing cultural circumstances and still be the Dharma? How realistic is it to imagine we can ever reproduce in our contemporary lives the training and experience of our ancestors?

The tensions held in these questions can cause our Dharmic Third to break down into the complementarity of arguments over authenticity. Obviously when we are engaged in learning a practice or ritual, we must learn the right and wrong way to bow or offer incense as it is practiced within our particular group. But when, within the larger community or among different sanghas or lineages, there is a preoccupation with authenticity, a certitude that our way is the one true way, that no teacher is as enlightened as our teacher, that others are simply benighted, deluded, watered-down versions of the real thing that we alone possess, then the Dharma has fallen into an egoistically preoccupied state of "I've got it and you don't." We should have no problem recognizing the authenticity of different practices, lineages, and religions. The authenticity of one does not preclude the authenticity of another. Indeed, the very act of recognizing the legitimacy of other teachers and teachings is a way of letting go of our self-centeredness and any residual feelings we may harbor about our own specialness or uniqueness.

When I think of the state of the Dharma in America, I find I must say yes to it *whole*—which is to say I admit that its history, like all history, is a *tragic* whole. If we look at the history of the American Civil War, we see on one hand horrific carnage and loss of life and on the other a series of events that, in the name of preserving the Union, also resulted in the ending of slavery. What does it mean to ask, "Was it worth it?" Was the Civil War a "good or just war"? In some sense, the question asks us to perform a thought experiment in which we imagine whether or not the good outcome, the ending of slavery, could have been accomplished without the terrible loss of life the actual war entailed. If we think we can easily imagine there was a nonviolent, political means to end slavery that was ignored or not considered, we may say that the war was a terrible mistake. But if we think, no, slavery wouldn't have ended in the United States for another generation or two or three, how can we weigh the cost in life against that goal? Perhaps what we long for is a utilitarian calculus that will give us an answer: What price is fair, reasonable, sane to pay for the end of slavery?

In Dostoyevsky's *The Brothers Karamazov* we are asked to consider whether the whole order and existence of the universe is "worth" the painful death of a single innocent child. The history of

Zen in America is not just tragic, but it is not simply the triumph of the Dharma coming to the West either. The tragic elements of the story are real and reflect the complications that arose at a particular historical moment, when a culture sick of its own materialism was susceptible to uncritical reverence of anyone who held out a spiritual alternative. It is the product of a time that was prone to conflate spiritual and sexual and political liberation and indulge in utopian countercultural fantasies. And it was, like the Renaissance, a time of an enormously fruitful intermingling and cross-pollination between cultures.

There is no Zen apart from Zen teachers. Preserving and honoring the Dharma in the abstract should not be a way of distancing ourselves from the failure of so many teachers. There is no way to say that the transmission of Zen to the West is "worth" the abuse of a single student. Isaiah Berlin adopted as a title for one of his books a quotation from Kant that he translates, "Out of the crooked timber of humanity no straight thing has ever been made." The Dharma, here and elsewhere, can be no exception. The lives of our teachers are crooked, sometimes in an endearing way, the way Shunryu Suzuki could call himself "a crooked cucumber"—but also sometimes crooked in a way that is actually criminal.

The realization of emptiness and interconnectedness by human beings does not, it seems, reliably transform them into something more than human. (It doesn't, I'm sorry to say, even reliably turn them into good human beings.) The fantasy that it always does, or even ever could, is one of the most effective curtains behind which our modern-day Wizards of Oz can hide. Anyone who tells you that Zen or any other practice will once and for all totally transform character is lying to you, and maybe to themselves as well.

And it's no good to claim transgressors aren't "really" enlightened. Closer to the truth may be the fact that "enlightenment" just isn't all that it's cracked up to be. I've met too many Zen teachers to think otherwise. (Of course, neither is psychoanalysis, but psychoanalysts are much less likely to be put on as high a pedestal these days . . .) If somewhere out there, in some temple in Japan or on a mountaintop in Tibet, there is a teacher who is "really" thoroughly and totally enlightened, it almost doesn't matter. I want to know and work with the students I have, with their occasional garden variety realizations (like my own . . .), and find out what this practice does and doesn't do for people like me.

The practice of Zen is a beautiful, transformative, profound, imperfect, unreliable, corruptible, culturally conditioned tradition and way of life of which I am part and which I am responsible for maintaining and passing on. The medium is the message: there is no Zen apart from Zen teachers and Zen students, doing what they do, devising ever new recipes for brewing the dregs we all need to live and practice.

CHAPTER SIX

IDEALIZATION

HUI-NENG AND THE ORIGINAL FACE

The story of the Sixth Ancestor, Hui-neng, offers us, even more than most stories of the lives of the ancient masters, an exemplary portrait of enlightenment. It is so exemplary, in fact, that some scholars have insinuated that not only has the portrait of the master been idealized but that the character of Hui-neng may have been fabricated out of whole cloth by a later generation seeking to anchor their own questionable claims of legitimacy to a renowned ancestor.

Hui-neng, as he (allegedly) recounts the story of his life at the beginning of the Platform Sutra, was an illiterate woodcutter's son who became instantly enlightened upon hearing a few verses of the Diamond Sutra being chanted. After all, in a tradition that defines itself as a "special transmission outside the scriptures, not dependent or words or phrases," what greater credential could there be than illiteracy?

Hui-neng comes at a pivotal point in the Chinese Zen lineage. From Bodhidharma through the Fifth Ancestor, Hongren, we have a single line of transmission, a single successor entrusted with the robe and bowl of Bodhidharma. Hui-neng is the last Dharma ancestor to be called a "Patriarch," and he is the last to receive the robe handed down from Bodhidharma. His teachings are called a *sutra*, a word otherwise reserved for the Indian texts recounting the Buddha's own words. Aspects of Hui-neng's biography closely match those traditionally attributed to Confucius, linking him to an archetype of Chinese virtue and giving credence to Zen as a home-grown, thoroughly Chinese product, no longer an exotic Indian import. The "Hui-neng" portrayed in the texts created centuries after his death was deliberately crafted to be an archetype of Chinese Zen, and it is not hard to be suspicious that his story is too good to be true.

Perhaps we have to be ready to hold two pictures in mind whenever we think of our founding fathers. There is the George Washington who cannot tell a lie and the rail-splitting Abe Lincoln, and then there are the real-life historical figures, still admirable, but more ambiguous in their real-life complexity. Yet as much as we say we know the difference between the legends and real life, we continue to feel disillusioned, if not betrayed, when our political leaders turn out to have feet of clay. We have a complex and conflicted relationship with our archetypes.

On the one hand, as Heinz Kohut taught us, they are the developmentally vital embodiments of our ideals and aspiration. But on the other, they can create a standard that it is impossible for any mortal to live up to. We may react to that gap in a variety of ways: within ourselves with a chronic sense of falling short; in others, especially figures we once hoped would live up to our idealization, with profound hurt, a sense of betrayal and anger. If we can see this phenomenon played out every day in the news coverage of our political figures, how much more so is it evoked when it comes to our religious leaders? The tragedy of so many American Zen teachers' fall from grace through sexual scandal is not just the undoubted harm done to the victims themselves but the way our idealized image of the "Zen master" has been defaced and our trust destroyed. It is not enough to say we need to "grow up" and be realistic about our teachers the way we all have had to do with our parents. The process of idealization is at once both a necessary and a normal part of our growth and a potentially destructive and delusive siren call to follow charismatic leaders down some very dangerous garden paths.

How we respond to the de-idealization of teachers is an important part of our practice.

One psychological maneuver that we all seem to deploy to one degree or another in response to the trauma of de-idealization is to remake the object of our idealization into an abstraction rather than a person. Thus, a teacher's personal life may be in shambles and he may have sexually and financially exploited an entire generation of students, but his "Dharma" is nonetheless genuine and somehow remains pure and untainted by his conduct. This is a complex, multidetermined psychological maneuver, one which can have, depending on the individual and the circumstances, both restorative and defensive aspects. As a way of recovering from trauma, for instance, a person may reestablish faith in the existence of the Dharma—or justice, or love—even though he or she has been badly injured by the behavior of a particular teacher or lover. This allows the Dharma to be preserved in the realm of the Third—a space beyond "doer and done-to"—where practice itself is not irrevocably tainted by the misconduct of any one individual.

Sometimes, however, this move into abstraction is primarily defensive. In this scenario, I vow never to allow myself to be dependent, trusting, or otherwise vulnerable to another human being ever again. Here the abstract Dharma functions in the service of dissociation, a splitting off of practice from vulnerability. We restore safety, but at the price of disconnection. I have had students who, having had bad experiences with a previous teacher, devote themselves to sitting, but who avoid dokusan and any personal relationship with me as a teacher. Zazen becomes a dissociated bubble of safety, an island retreat. This may be an unavoidable first step, but it leads to a life in limbo and needs to be recognized for what it is when the time is right.

So how should we make use of the story of an idealized figure like the Sixth Ancestor? Even if we accept the academic assertion that the Platform Sutra is a later generation forgery concocted to establish a patronage claim for another teacher, Shen-hui, the forger sure knew what he was doing. For the text of the Platform Sutra not only gives us the portrait of an idealized ancestor, it is a powerful lesson in the Dharma in its own right, one that has outlived the complexities surrounding its creation. What does it teach us?

The first lesson is exemplified by the poem Hui-neng writes (or has written out for him, since he is supposed to have been illiterate) in response to one written by the head monk. The Fifth Ancestor has asked everyone to compose a verse expressing their understanding, and on the basis of what they write he will choose his successor. The head monk (who is identified in the Platform Sutra as none other than the Shen-xiu, with whom Shen-hui was in competition) composed this verse:

> The body is the Bodhi tree,
> The mind is like a clear mirror.
> At all times we must strive to polish it.
> And must not let the dust collect.

Hui-neng in response wrote:

> Originally there is no tree of enlightenment,
> Nor is there a stand with a clear mirror.
> From the beginning not one thing exists;
> Where, then, is a grain of dust to cling?

How do we understand the metaphors of the bright mirror and dust in the context of our own practice? The mirror, for most of us, will represent some form of clarity, a state of mind to which we aspire. What then counts as dust? For many people in many different meditation traditions, thought itself is dust, and the continual wiping away of thought, by means of pure concentration or through the use of a dust-cloth mantra, is the most basic form of practice. From that perspective, the deep silence behind or beyond our thoughts is itself the true nature that we seek, and practice is an endless process of removing discursive contaminants. Modern students may not seek that degree of mental purity through the elimination of thoughts, but when it comes to emotion, their underlying motivation may be quite similar. Anger, anxiety, and depression are typically what we nowadays identify as the "dust" we want to wipe off our mental mirror.

We presume there is a state of equanimity hidden under a layer of emotional detritus that we want practice to clear away. But Hui-neng's poem directly counters that view, regardless of how we conceive of the dust that clouds our mind-mirror. Both the mirror and the dust itself are empty, he assures us, so what is there to obscure or be obscured? What this says, in essence, is that our thoughts and emotions are not defilements separate or in some sense layered on top of our otherwise clear minds. Thoughts and emotions are not defiling our minds, they *are* our mind. We need not remove them but only see them for what they are. Practice, in effect, goes from an endless, and usually endlessly futile, endeavor to "clean up" our mind to the understanding that our mind is already intrinsically clear because intrinsically empty. *The mind cannot be defiled by its contents.* Our task is not to *create* this state of affairs but to see it is already here.

Needless to say, Hui-neng won the Fifth Ancestor's approval for his poem and received the robe of transmission in a secret nighttime ceremony. The ceremony was conducted in secret because Hui-neng, who had spent all his time at the monastery working as a layman pounding rice, was not ordained and did not take part in the regular daily practice of the monks. He would have seemed a completely unacceptable choice to most of the community and they would literally try to get the robe back and undo the transmission to this outsider.

It is part of Hui-neng's story, for better or worse, that "practice" as we usually understand it—neither zazen or monastic life and ritual—played no part in his attaining or perfecting his realization. He exemplified the school of "sudden" (as opposed to "gradual") enlightenment—in an instant one can "see" reality with perfect clarity. Like suddenly seeing a new aspect of an ambiguous-image illusion, it is right there in front of you, where it has been all along. What does practice have to do with it? Can you prepare or train yourself to see?

In any case, the most persistent of the pursuing monks, named Ming, had been a general in his premonastic life. Hui-neng placed the robe on a rock between them and offered it to Ming, saying the Dharma was not something to be grasped or fought over.

Startled, Ming was unable to move a muscle. Hui-neng then asks him, "Right now, thinking neither good nor evil, what is your original face before your parents were born?"

With this Ming has a sudden realization, yet still part of him wonders, "Besides what I have just seen is there any further mystery?" Hui-neng replies that what he has seen is not a mystery at all and urges him to return to the monastery and remain the disciple of the Fifth Ancestor.

This narrative, as recounted by Hui-neng himself at the beginning of the Platform Sutra, dramatically presents many elements that have characterized Zen ever since. Like Ming, students come to practice thinking there is something outside themselves to "get"—

maybe not as literally as getting a robe, but something to pursue, something the other has that they desperately want. But is what we want outside or inside? The koan of the original face turns the tables and reveals the other side of our fantasy. Of course, what I am looking for isn't *outside*, so it must be *inside*, deep inside, hidden away, like a buried treasure that I need to uncover. What is my *original* face? What mysterious essence do I contain that is not conditioned, not the result of my own personal history, not, we might say nowadays, a result of my genetic or developmental history?

But looking inside is as much a mistake as looking outside.

What is the alternative to something being neither on the inside or the outside? Where else is there?

As is the case with many koans, what we are looking for is hidden in plain sight, hidden in the very words of the question itself. Hui-neng asks, "This very moment, thinking neither good nor evil, what is your original face?" "This very moment"—is that inside or outside?

"Thinking neither good nor evil,"—that is, not thinking at all, not framing, not judging, not knowing—where is your original face? Do you have two? Is the one on your head a copy of the real thing?

There a song by the Grateful Dead about a character so slick he could "steal your face right off of your head." That's what we do to ourselves when we lose trust in the completeness of this very moment, when we allow ourselves to be bewitched into thinking there is something missing that we have to go looking for. The language of koans skillfully taps into this psychology of *lack*, bringing right up to the surface our unconscious fears of being less than whole, and forces us to look everywhere for our own head, until the moment comes when we can be sure that it has been sitting on top of our shoulders all along. We might say this is the Zen equivalent of Freud's metaphor of penis envy, which he formulated to describe that same sense of intrinsic lack he imagined was part of every little girl's psychic development. Probably Freud's mistake was attributing penis envy only to girls: we *all* grow up thinking something is missing—if not between our legs, then between our ears.

The problem of getting stuck looking either inside or outside when where we need to be is right on the surface, right in the ever changing present moment, is reflected in our confusion about the whole notion of *depth*, in both its religious and psychological meanings. The Trappist monk Thomas Merton, after many decades of writing about our true nature, finally concluded, "The time has probably come to go back on all that I have said about one's 'true self,' etc etc. And show that there is after all no hidden mysterious 'real self' OTHER THAN or 'hiding behind' the self that one is . . ." Even though a central tenet of Buddhism has always been that nothing—no dharma, no thing, no person, so self—has any intrinsic unchanging essence, generations of Buddhists have misconstrued the idea of buddha nature to mean just that—an inner essence, an inner potential for realization, a inner true self—that practice is designed to uncover and cultivate.

Hui-neng's question about your original face is echoed in the first of three barriers set up by Master Tou-shuai (Jap. Tosotsu):

> Monks, you search through the abandoned grasses, leave no stone unturned to explore the depths, simply to see into your True Nature. Now I want to ask you, just at this moment: where is your true nature?

Once again, we need to ask what does depth have to do with our true nature? Pointedly Tou-shuai asks, *where* will we look for this true nature? This is a case in which, instead of trying to turn our gaze to follow the pointing finger up into the sky, all the way to the moon, we should stop and look directly at the finger itself and forget all about the moon.

True nature erupts from the very first word of question itself, and there is no gap between searching and finding. True nature searches for true nature and there is nowhere for it to hide.

Another name for all those "abandoned grasses" might be our ordinary mind, in its unruly "natural" state. Is the goal of practice to turn our mind into a carefully raked and trimmed Japanese garden? If so, we will follow a path of meticulous mindfulness but forever be subject to the vicissitudes of what is uncontrollable, breaking in on us from the outside and bursting forth from our unconscious. An old master is said, upon visiting one of those perfectly maintained gardens, to have complimented the monk in charge on his work, saying only one thing was lacking: whereupon he shook the branches of an overhanging tree, randomly scattering leaves across the perfectly raked surface.

We find our true nature down in the grasses, not by gazing up at the moon. Or better yet, we come to see the grasses best by moonlight. Nothing is changed, except how they are illuminated. Will we see them as beautiful in their natural state or as unruly and in constant need of control and correction?

Students who have had some glimpse of the moon, some taste of realization, often get stuck wanting more, wanting yet another, longer glimpse of that pure beautiful light. Sadly, I would say the majority of students get stuck for a long time at this point, sometimes for the rest of their lives. Having had a certain experience, they forever contrast that experience with the rest of their ordinary consciousness and live in the grip of an insidious new dualism, forever comparing, forever longing.

Sometimes I think that whole Zen centers have been built on this particular plateau, their students forever tantalized by something once glimpsed, but forever just out of reach. Teachers themselves can collude with this mindset. When we say "not yet, not yet" we must be clear that this isn't an expression of endless striving for self-improvement or "complete" realization. Rather, there is nothing final; that incompleteness, the tangle of wild grasses, is not separate from completeness. Someone once asked Joko whether she thought she would ever attain *annutara-samyak-sambodhi* (supreme, unsurpassed, perfect enlightenment) in this life. "I hope the thought never crosses my mind," she replied.

What I've called "seeing the grasses by moonlight" is just another way of saying our ordinary mind is the way. Nothing is missing. Nothing is hidden.

CHAPTER SEVEN

APPEARANCE & REALITY

THE PHYSICAL BODY

A monk asked Ta-lung (Jap. Dairyu), "The physical body is disintegrating, but what about the immutable spiritual body?"

Ta-lung said, "The autumn foliage of the mountains spreads like brocade; the water in the valley remains blue as indigo."

Like the pursuit of our original face, the pursuit of an immutable spiritual body that is "behind" or somehow underlies and forms an unchanging foundation to this changing world ultimately leads us to the realization that what the appearances of things are concealing is the fact that there is nothing (or no-thing) behind them; consequently they are not "mere" appearances at all. There is no essential bedrock to be found whether we look deep inside or behind the curtain. Yet the meaning or clarity or luminosity we have been seeking is not therefore absent from our lives or from the world. It is just that, caught up in our search, we have been relentless in overlooking where it has been hiding in plain sight all along. In *Confessions of a Buddhist Atheist*, Stephen Batchelor describes Buddha's awakening as "a radical shift in perspective, rather than the gaining of privileged knowledge into some higher truth." It is not as if he saw something new, so much as he saw what we all see, this ever-changing world, in a new light.

Ta-lung answers the monk with images from the ever-changing world, the world of appearances: beauty of the autumn foliage, the color of flowing water. The monk's question is grounded in a basic dualist assumption, or perhaps we should say a basic human longing: that the world of impermanence, of change and decay, should not be the only world that there is. The traditional Mahayana triad of *dharmakaya*, *sambhogakaya*, and *nirmanakaya*—the three "bodies" of a buddha—are ways of viewing this one world from three different aspects. The metaphorical body of the Buddha, referred to in the monk's question to Ta-lung, is said to reflect these three aspects.

The *dharmakaya* is the Absolute, the essence of the universe, the unity of all things and beings that exists whether realized or not. The *nirmanakaya* is the earthly, physical body of a buddha, which manifests in the world to teach the Dharma and bring all beings to enlightenment. For example, the historical Buddha, Shakyamuni, is said to have been a nirmanakaya buddha. The nirmanakaya body is subject to sickness, old age, and death like any other living being. Sambhogakaya is the body of bliss, or the body that experiences the fruits of Buddhist practice. It is sometimes explained as the communion of the Absolute (dharmakaya) with the relative (nirmanakaya), where the relative body experiences the bliss of realization of the Absolute. However, these distinctions are themselves the result of our imagination, our capacity for abstraction and to give different names to different aspects of our experience. Ta-lung's answer literally brings the monk back to earth, a gentle reminder not to concretize or try to take literally the figments of our metaphysical imagination.

There is only one world, one life. From what vantage point are we looking? Looked at from different directions, it can take on different guises, and we can give those guises different names.

I often invoke the ambiguous image of the duck-rabbit. That image may be seen as either the head of a duck or the head of a rabbit. To only see the duck or only see the rabbit is like seeing one aspect of the buddha-body and not the others. We are not wrong, but our vision is incomplete. The question of what is involved in seeing a figure like this one way or another, and what happens when we shift perspectives, was taken up by Ludwig Wittgenstein in his *Philosophical Investigations*.

For Wittgenstein, the shift in perspective involves not only a sudden recognition of a rabbit where before we only saw a duck but also an awareness that our perception is being shaped by a perspective. Here is Wittgenstein imagining how we try to make sense of what goes on when this happens:

When I see the figure for the first time, I might simply say, "It's a picture of the head of a rabbit." I wouldn't say, "Now I'm seeing it as the head of a rabbit," anymore than, looking at the table, I would say, "I'm seeing it as a table."

The change of aspect. "But surely you would say that the picture is altogether different now!"

But what is different: my impression? My point of view?—Can I say? I describe the alteration like a perception; quite as if the object had altered before my eyes.

What the duck-rabbit figure shows us is not that it's easy to confuse ducks with rabbits but rather a single image can truly be said to represent either a duck or a rabbit. Like life itself, it is a single thing that can be seen in different ways, each of which is indisputably true, and yet to see it only one way is incomplete.

The expression of a change of aspect is the expression of a *new* perception and at the same time of the perception being unchanged. Both before and after realization, mountains are mountains and rivers are rivers. And yet *after* feels different than *before*.

"I meet someone whom I have not seen for years; I see him clearly, but fail to know him. Suddenly I know him, I see the old face in the altered one," writes Wittgenstein. Compare this to Wu-men's description of realization as like suddenly seeing your own father—there's no question of whether or not you recognize him. Yet "our father" has been standing in front of us all along. Life has been presenting itself to us, and yet we have failed to recognize, failed to perceive some aspect of it that is neither hidden nor apparent.

When we go from seeing the glass as half empty to seeing it as half full, what has changed? Perhaps we might say it's our *mood* that has changed, rather than our actual perception. The world feels, as well as looks, different.

Like the duck and rabbit, the dharmakaya and the nirmanakaya are in fact the same, but looked at from different perspectives. It is as if "ducks" represented everything good and true and beautiful in our lives, while "rabbits" were symbols of everything false, dangerous, or unpleasant. And suddenly, we saw they were in fact the same, not two species but one—and like the drawing, the creatures themselves were actually one animal that, because we observed it in two different settings, under two different conditions, we had mistaken for separate species. The experience of seeing both aspects of duck/rabbit at once, of seeing that there is only one world that is simultaneously the world of wonder and the world of suffering—what we can call the world of sambhogakaya—both changes everything and changes nothing.

CHAPTER EIGHT

CHANGE & UNITY

KUEI-SHAN'S BUFFALO

Kuei-shan (Jap. Isan) said to his students, "Two hundred years after I'm dead, a water buffalo will be born in this valley with the words I am Kuei-shan on its side. Tell me, would you call it a buffalo or would you call it Kuei-shan?"

Many contemporary psychoanalytic theorists, like Philip Bromberg, are increasingly becoming comfortable with a view of the self as a "multiplicity of discontinuous self-states . . . a set of discrete, more or less overlapping schemata that, taken together, define who one is—each schema being organized around a particular self-other configuration with a distinctive affective flavoring."

This picture of discontinuous self-states does not imply that psychoanalysts are all suddenly becoming mystics. One can understand this model in very ordinary terms: think of the person you are when you're around your spouse and then who you are around your mother. For most of us, a rather sudden shift in feeling and identity takes place when we switch from one relationship to another. Certainly, I know my teenage son is very different person around me than he is around his friends. Yet, how different? How much do we remain the same person as we switch roles and self-states? How many of "me" are there?

In a remarkable—though, as it turns out, fictitious—account of a meeting between Charles Dickens and Fyodor Dostoyevsky, biographer Claire Tomalin wrote that Dickens told Dostoyevsky:

> All the good simple people in his novels, Little Nell, even the holy simpletons like Barnaby Rudge, are what he wanted to have been, and his villains were what he was (or rather what he found in himself), his cruelty, his attacks of causeless enmity toward those who were helpless and looked to him for comfort, his shrinking from those he ought to love. . . . There were two people in him, he told me: one who feels as he ought to feel and one who feels the opposite. "From the one who feels the opposite I make my evil characters, from the one who feels as a man ought to feel I try to live my life."
>
> "Only two people?" I asked.

In this fable, Dickens is able to accept the fact that he contains opposites. Dostoyevsky can go further and, like Walt Whitman, say, "I contain multitudes."

Being able to hold separate different aspects of our self, being able to tolerate the difference and even the conflicts that arise between who we are in different contexts and with different people, is an example of *ordinary* or *healthy dissociation*. Our ordinary, and basically healthy, way of experiencing the shifts we undergo as we shift roles and states is to experience and tolerate a certain degree of awkwardness and conflict. We can recognize how we suddenly revert to an old childish way of being when we go home for the holidays, one at odds with our usual mature way of being around friends and colleagues. There might be a sheepish acknowledgment that we are falling into old patterns or that our mothers can still "push our buttons." But, most of the time we can tolerate holding the two versions of ourselves in mind at once and feel the conflict.

In the words of Philip Bromberg:

> Self-states are what the mind comprises. Dissociation is what the mind does. The relationship between self-states and dissociation is what the mind is. It is the stability of that relationship that enables a person to experience continuity as "I." A flexible relationship among self-states through the use of ordinary dissociation is what allows a human being to engage the ever-shifting requirements of life's complexities with creativity and spontaneity.

Our lives are about change, about how we change as the world around us changes, but also about how we experience a sense of continuity throughout changing circumstances. When I change, am I still the same person? Is there some core sense of my "self" that continues to exist no matter what happens to me?

Taking a cue from Kuei-shan, if I turned into a buffalo would I still be "me"? What could it possibly mean to still be "Kuei-shan" in the body of a water buffalo?

Kuei-shan invites us to move freely with creativity and sponta-neity in response to his question. How shall we understand these different states of "Kuei-shan" and "buffalo"? How do we express both continuity and change?

The dramatic shift from "Kuei-shan" to "buffalo" illustrates the feeling of (almost) total otherness that can accompany the shift of one self-state in relation to another, even in what is fundamentally healthy dissociation. Each self-state feels like a complete identity in its own right, and yet our mind is made of a wide variety of such states, some of which seem to bear very little resemblance to the others. Kuei-shan uses the metaphor of reincarnation to illustrate how profound the gap between states can feel.

Shohaku Okamura, in his masterful book *Living by Vow*, has remarked that while he doesn't believe that we transmigrate from one life to another, he's certain we all transmigrate *within* this life, which is a nice way of describing our shift from one self-state to another. Yet the shift isn't total; the buffalo is still called Kuei-shan and all my self-states answer to the name Barry. We are not, here, in Dr. Jekyll and Mr. Hyde territory, where one part of the self is totally alien and unknown to the others. If we think of the buffalo as being the animal from the famous Ox-Herding pictures, we can imagine that the buffalo represents buddha nature that takes on different guises, sometimes called Kuei-shan, sometimes called buffalo, according to circumstances. That way of approaching the buffalo leads us toward the assumption that there's some sort of continuous underlying essence, whether we call it buddha nature or the soul, that transmigrates and appears in different forms.

There is a saying "Wherever you go, there you are." We intuitively feel the truth of that statement—there's something of ourselves, our perspective, our experience that we bring to each new situation. No matter how different the experience, we want to say it's still "my" experience. One side of the experience of being in psychoanalysis or practicing meditation is to see how much we unconsciously configure our subjective experience of the new situation along old lines—one aspect of what analysts call transference is the way we experience the people in our present lives in some way as replays of old scenarios we enacted with our parents and siblings. We come to new relationships primed with old hopes and fears—all the things we've learned over the years to expect in the way of satisfaction or disappointment from others.

Unless we begin to recognize those patterns, we may be destined never to have any new experiences at all. We can feel like we got stuck in an endless rerun of scenes from all past, where for instance "men are always abusive and can't be trusted (like my father)" or "what I really need is complete attention and unconditional love (like I always wished for from my mother)." If we are stuck in old patterns, the one thing that remains constant in the midst of life's changes is indeed our "self," but it is the constancy of stuck-ness, a constancy born out of a blindness to the potential for the new. It is a paradox in the Buddhist idea of impermanence that, though everything changes, I can still feel so stuck in my own unhappiness.

Kuei-shan's buffalo suggests another kind of interplay between constancy and change—what relation do changes in my body have to my sense of my self? Kuei-shan asks would he still be Kuei-shan if he were reborn as a water buffalo—one with a big hint painted on its side as to just who was reborn. If we literally try to imagine it, it's hard to know where to begin. Should we picture Kuei-shan's human consciousness "inside" a body of the buffalo? That would be a horrifying scenario, like the character in Kafka's story who wakes up inside the body of a giant cockroach. Yet we all wake up one day to find ourselves inside a body that has changed dramatically—that is what aging does to us. I remember my mother, when she turned seventy, telling me it felt very strange to be seventy because she felt that she was still the young woman she had been forty or fifty years previously, but now she was "in" this old body. In another way, it's what my son is going through as he enters puberty—all of a sudden the kid he feels himself to be is "in" a body that is doing some very strange things.

Contrast the saying "Wherever you go, there you are" with Heraclitus's maxim "You can't step into the same river twice." Not only is the river different moment by moment, so are you. It's a curious fact that both sayings have the ring of truth, and yet what they are saying is exactly opposite to one another. When we hear them said separately, we feel each captures something very true and very basic about our experience of our "self." Yet when we put them side by side, they seem to contradict one another. How can that be?

The fact that they both feel right tells us something important about the "self" that they are trying to describe, a lesson that we have to learn over and over again in many different ways and from many different directions. The "self" is not a single "thing" with a list of attributes that we can be right or wrong about. We confuse ourselves by unwittingly shifting from an account of a particular self-state, to a description of the mind that contains varying self-states, to the person who is both a body and mind—all of these at one time or another we refer to as my "self." We have to get used to the idea that we use the word "self" in many different contexts, put it to different uses in those different contexts, and that its meaning is as fluid as those contexts and uses. To study the self is to study the language of the self.

It is a very common figure of speech to say that "I" exist "in" my body. For as much as we may intellectually assent to the idea that I am not separate from my body, that there is no such thing as a qualitatively separate nonmaterial essence called the soul or spirit or buddha nature riding around in the material container of the body—at some level it just feels that way, doesn't it? Dualism has been such a persistent philosophical and religious concept because it does in fact describe how it feels for most of us to "have" a body. An idea that has been around for thousands of years can't just be "wrong" in an easily dismissed way—we have to see the way it fits our experience so closely that we are very reluctant to give it up, or feel the need for an alternative way of seeing things.

We might compare it to the view the ancients held that the sun and the stars all revolved around the earth. If you look at the sun moving across the sky from morning to night it's a perfectly reasonable thing to assume. There's a story that Wittgenstein once said to a colleague he couldn't understand why people persisted so long in thinking that the sun revolved around the earth. His colleague, not knowing what to say, blurted out, "But that's just how it looks." To which Wittgenstein replied, "But how would it look if the earth revolved around the sun?" Of course it would look exactly the same way (since it does), but it may take a long time and a willingness to actually look at new evidence to convince us to see things in a new way.

What would it look or feel like if instead of my self being "in" my body, my self *was* my body?

Since it is, it would have to feel just the way it already does, including that dualistic sense of *insideness*, which is evidently a characteristic of a body capable of consciousness—that is to say, one of the subjective "feels" of consciousness is a sensation of consciousness arising inside, of my self being inside my body. That sense of insideness can't just be "wrong"—we have to take it as a given of our subjective experience. That's just what it feels like, just like it *still* looks like the sun revolves around the earth even after we learned that it's the other way around.

In the koan, the dualisms of change and permanence, body and mind, inside and outside, human and animal are encapsulated into the question: Will you call that buffalo Kuei-shan or not? In order to correctly answer the question, the students are expected not only to grow horns and a tail but to make them genuinely their own.

That's because one way Zen demonstrates a path out of a seemingly insoluble dualistic impasse or paradox is through *play*. If a question doesn't have a logical answer, perhaps the problem is in the logic, not in the question. Wittgenstein famously remarked that a book of philosophy could be written that was made up entirely of jokes. A collection of Zen koans perhaps fulfills that possibility even better than he could have imagined. Whereas for Freud, jokes allowed the eruption of a forbidden wish into consciousness, for Wittgenstein, jokes marked the eruption of nonsense into logic. Jokes demarcated the limits of sense, of what could be logically said. (His *Tractatus Logico-Philosophicus* likewise traced the boundary between sense and nonsense in a slightly more formal way . . .)

Zen koans can feel like jokes we don't get; we don't see how to break out of the paradox into a playful space where the dualisms all vanish. It's not by chance that a teacher sometimes recognizes whether a student has really "answered" a koan correctly by the laughter that comes with realization. Step outside of yourself and (especially if you are an impeccably proper, that is to say uptight, Japanese monk) show me how you can become that girl across the room—"Is she the younger or older sister?" Playing charades, we lose our inhibitions, which is to say we drop something of our social self and our social sense of shame and, in response to such koans, play at being anything at all. But if I can be anything at all, what is left of "me"?

CHAPTER NINE

TRAUMATIC DISSOCIATION

CH'IEN AND HER SOUL ARE SEPARATED

*Wu-tsu (Jap. Goso) asked a monk, "Ch'ien (Jap. Sei-jo)
and her soul were separated, which is the true one?"*

This koan is based on an old Chinese folk story, which Wu-tsu is
using to make a point about the nature of the true self. To sum-
marize the story: Ch'ien is a young woman who grew up in a little
village along with her childhood sweetheart, and the two of them
always assumed that when they grew up they would be married. But
when Ch'ien came of age, her father picked out a different husband
for her and told her she couldn't marry her sweetheart. Thereupon,
her boyfriend left town, because he couldn't bear her marrying
someone else. He got on a boat and sailed down the river. But after
he had gone a short way, he suddenly saw someone following him
along the bank and pulled over. Miraculously, it was Ch'ien, who
had somehow managed to follow him. She got into his boat and
they sailed away to a far off country where they married and had
children. Years passed and Ch'ien missed her old father, whom they
had left behind in their home town and who had never seen his
grandchildren. And so she said to her husband, "I can't just stay
here and not know whether he is alive or dead. We must go back

and make our peace with him." So they got in the boat and sailed back to their hometown. And her husband now says to her, "You stay in the boat, and I will go meet with your father and explain the situation and then you can come out." So he goes in and explains how he and Ch'ien ran off so many years ago and how they are now happily married with children and how she wants to be reunited with him. And old father looks at him as if he is nuts, "I don't know what you are talking about, Ch'ien never left home. The day you left she fell sick and has been lying in bed there motionless for all these years." The husband says, "No, no, she's out in the boat, she is with me right now." So the father brings him to the bedroom and sure enough Ch'ien is lying in bed. But then the husband goes out to the boat and brings his Ch'ien back into the house. When Ch'ien walks into the room where her other self is lying in bed, somehow, miraculously, the part that has been sick all these years gets up, the two of them come together, and they merge and become one person. And (presumably) live happily ever after. So Wu-tsu asks: all those years Ch'ien and her soul were separated—when she was split in half—which was the real one?

If Kuei-shan's buffalo can offer a playful approach to the normal dissociation of everyday life, the sometimes fluid, sometimes dramatic changes in self-states we all undergo as we "transmigrate" through different roles, moods, and relations, then the story of Ch'ien confronts us with the more drastic, more discontinuous forms of dissociation that can result from trauma. For although at the level of the koan both Ch'ien and the buffalo can be approached playfully and mimetically, Ch'ien's story, despite its fairy-tale ending, is one in which a parent's utter disregard for his child's need for love leads to her falling desperately ill and portrays what happens when we are cut off from a vital part of ourselves. This way of talking about the koan would of course seem irrelevant to Wu-men, the compiler of the Gateless Gate, and to generations of traditional Zen teachers, for whom the emotional level is just a distraction from the underlying essential truth of the koan. But bypassing the emotional in order to get at the essential is how Zen can become lopsided, so I will concentrate on what is usually bypassed before going on to talk about the story from the more traditional perspective.

Often people come to Zen practice because they have lost touch with something vital in themselves and are trying to bring it back. They rightly see that practice can put them back in touch with their body, their feelings, their connection to others. Like Ch'ien, in a very literal sense, if we try to split off some vital part of who we are, we will fall sick. Ch'ien can't live without love, cannot live without marrying her sweetheart, and so she goes to bed, depressed and immobilized. But unfortunately, people can also use practice to rationalize having lost something and being cut off from it. They imagine practice will allow them to live without love (or hope, or physical comfort, or recognition, or any personal needs). They imagine it will somehow make them strong enough to do without those things.

We imagine that we can exile some aspect of ourselves through practice and still flourish. If we go that route, we end up like a ghost and then call being a ghost "being spiritual." But the bottom line is that we've lost something of our true self, our embodiment, and if we use practice to cut ourselves off from some aspect or another of our emotional reality, we have perverted practice and will eventually have to pay the price.

If we've lost touch with some aspect of ourselves, we must try to go and get it back. We can't be our true self if we are only half of our self. Yet the processes that have brought about the split are often unconscious and we may be only dimly aware that something is missing. How can we know? Like the background radiation that pervades every direction that scientists claim is residue of the Big Bang, so too we might say that our subjective experience of the *affective tone* of the world is the remnant of our early, sometimes preverbal, childhood experience. By *affective tone*, I mean how we might instinctively react to silence—is it frightening and empty, or serene and calming? Do we experience the open spaces of nature as lonely unpopulated expanses or are they enveloping and deeply enriching experiences? Do we find crowded city streets lively and stimulating or overwhelming, cacophonous, and looming? Do we approach each day with a sense of possibility, crowded with options, or as empty expanses of time to be filled and gotten through? There is something about such reports, sometimes deeply embedded in a person's unspoken intuitive sense of "that's just how the world is," that provides the color, tone, or, if you will, musical soundtrack to a person's life.

Affective tone can alert us to a history of trauma. Trauma can take many forms, from overt physical and sexual abuse to more subtle varieties of psychological intimidation or deprivation. Some forms of trauma leave obvious traces in a posttraumatic syndrome of flashbacks, nightmares, hyperarousal, and hypervigilance—others may have sequelae that are more subtle and center around a pervasive psychic numbing. Memories of trauma may be repressed and inaccessible by ordinary means of recollection. The emotional impact may be dissociated, so that while remembered, a person denies or minimizes the effect of the incidents. The experience of trauma may be literally unspeakable; no words can be found to convey what lies behind a pervasive sense of sadness, damage, badness, guilt, shame, chronic anxiety, avoidance, or self-destructive behaviors. Any one of these symptoms asks us to look deeper and inquire when and how these feelings became a part of the world we take for granted.

Among the possible consequences of some forms of trauma (such as sexual abuse) is the subjective sense that it is an intrinsically private, unshareable, sometimes literally unspeakable experience that has separated a person off from the rest of normal life. Furthermore, the person feels left in a shame-ridden state defined by what has been *done to* them; rather than being defined by their own agency, they are the *object* of trauma. A person may feel defiled, contaminated, or to blame for what has happened. "I can never forgive myself for what was done to me," one patient told me. Being able to reimmerse one's self into what has been literally unspeakable is the necessary precursor of both treatment and genuine realization.

Psychoanalysts have needed to learn that no matter how hard they try to play the role of the "good" parent to a traumatized patient, their inevitable lapses of empathy or understanding will end up re-creating in the therapy echoes of the very trauma they are attempting to explore. Yet as analysts we have learned that to be part of the solution, we may first have to become part of the problem. When something cannot find a way to be said between the patient and analyst, often as not it will be enacted instead. Analysts have learned that they must own the attribution of retraumatizing the patient and not defend their good intentions or insist that the patient is mistaken about what has been going on.

This is unfortunately something that, in my experience, Zen teachers have been slow to learn—instead insisting on the rightness of their understanding and laying the blame for impasses on the defensiveness, attachment, or ego of the student. At one level, they may be right, but being right is one thing and being helpful is another.

Enactments, rather than constituting errors or failures in the treatment, actually allow the reexperiencing of the trauma to occur in a relational context where the unspeakable becomes speakable. Ideally koans can likewise give voice to aspects of our self that have lost their voice, and the fully embodied response the teacher demands that we give to the koan restores the possibility of agency, impact, acknowledgment, and repair instead of mute passivity, in a way that parallels the analytic Third's restoration of a meaningful and lawful relational world.

Although we normally associate the word trauma with a sudden damaging or abusive incident (whether within the family, like incest, or socially, like 9/11), clinically we are equally likely to encounter what Bromberg calls *developmental trauma*:

> a failure of responsiveness by the mother or father to some genuine aspect of the child's self, not necessarily open disapproval or abusiveness . . . but a masked withdrawal from authentic contact that leaves the child experiencing part of herself as having no pleasurable value to a loved other and, thus, no relational experience as part of "me." . . . The child's own need for loving recognition becomes despised and shame ridden. The need becomes a dissociated "not-me" aspect of self that, when triggered, releases not only unmet hunger for authentic responsiveness, but a flood of shame . . .

Frequently it is the parents' own shame and disavowal of aspects of their own need and aspects of their own emotional make-up that makes it impossible for them to see their child's corresponding needs. There is a thus a shame-ridden perpetuation of dissociation and disavowal from one generation to the next. Although the damage done by overt sexual misconduct on the part of Zen teachers has raised the most obvious questions about the validity of their own training and realization, it is perhaps the more insidious disavowal of emotional need that has pervaded—and perverted—traditional Zen training.

Teachers who themselves have come to practice to disengage from their own emotional lives, to transcend their own personal trauma, may convey to their students that any show of emotional need, let alone any "need for loving recognition," is a weakness incompatible with the rigors and reality of training. Like Ch'ien when deprived of her beloved, a student may wither into depression only to be told that her depression is further sign of her self-centered attachments, which if not somehow curbed will result in the further shame of being judged unsuitable for further training.

Sadly, the last thing that the teacher in this sort of situation can ever see or acknowledge is the role of his or her own behavior in inducing the student's difficulty. Part of the teacher's own dissociative process is to project all his or her own disavowed need, vulnerability, and emotionality onto the student, which, in the form of the student, then may be literally expelled from the Zen center. It has been my experience that when such students encounter a teacher who can help them work through their shame and who can view their emotional vulnerabilities as being no different than his or her own, a dramatic blossoming and flourishing may occur that gives lie to the previous teacher's assessment of the student's unsuitability for practice.

Although I have stressed the underlying traumatic aspect of Ch'ien's story, it is usually told as if it were another dramatic illustration of normal dissociation. Wu-men invites us to look at the span of many years the way Kuei-shan does the span of lifetimes. In each case, the long temporal gap symbolizes what is actually going on moment after moment. The depressed Ch'ien, the married Ch'ien, the one that is united. You could say that these are all different self-states that succeed one another. In the folk story, there is a gap of years, but we may go through them all in thirty seconds . . . a moment of feeling depressed, feeling bored, elated, perfectly calm, restless. Which one is the real you? If we experience all those different states while we are sitting, is there any one of them we can single out and say, this represents true practice? When you are sitting there all calm without a thought in your head or when the snot is dripping off your nose and you are wondering when this period is going to end? Which one is true practice? We pass through all of these states and inevitably we prefer one to the other. We want one of them to be the real thing and we want the other to be something that we can push into the background and eventually eliminate. We want to pick out one and say this is the real one.

What is our true self? Wu-men, in his comment on this case, may complicate matters when he uses the metaphor of a traveler going from inn to inn to describe Ch'ien going from one state to another. This image implies there is a single self experiencing one state, one inn, after another, whereas it might be truer to say that who we are also changes from inn to inn. That was Heraclitus's point when he said we cannot step into the same river twice. Not only is the river never the same but neither are we. Sometimes Wu-men's perspective is interpreted to mean that "our true self" is always present and unchanging regardless of circumstances. But what is that true self but emptiness itself? And if the true self is empty, then EMPTINESS + THE INN just equals THE INN. We *are* our next experience, not we *have* our next experience.

Though our ordinary way of speaking is to say there is one person who *has* experiences—i.e., I, Barry Magid, went to high school, then I went to college, then I went to medical school, and the same name appears on the degree granted by each successive institution—this koan tells us something is falsified in this straight-forward account. Who I am is always subtly changing and being changed by what is happening. The *me* that went to medical school was no longer the me that went to high school and is no longer who I am now. This is the part we all half get and half resist. How fluid do we allow ourselves to be, how much do we try to hold on to one constant state, one constant observer, one constant view of ourselves? By holding on to a view of an unchanging self, we may end up saying, "I sat really well this morning but badly this afternoon." But really who we are is just the experience of having it be one way in the morning and another way in the afternoon. You can't stand outside of that—well, we can!—but we end up like Ch'ien, split in half. And then one half tries to control the other, one half may even try to assassinate the other if we aren't able to tolerate that all these different states and feelings are who we are. One day the act of dying, like a crab hanging over a pot of boiling water in Wu-men's commentary, will be who we are. Where is your true self then?

The koan of Ch'ien presents a radically *horizontal* picture of the self: one state lies alongside another, and there is no basis to say one is more real or truer than the other. Wu-men's verse at the end of this case however, reminds us that there are two ways of looking at the world, through the lens of sameness and the lens of differentiation:

The moon and the clouds are the same;
mountains and valleys are different.

Some years ago, Joseph Campbell became famous for telling people to "follow their bliss." Naturally, we all strive to be true to what feels most authentic about us; we want to nourish the parts of us that are artistic, creative, imaginative, compassionate, altruistic, and so on. We can feel we spend too much time compromising and being accommodative, too restricted by artificial social norms. We may be afraid that we've created a false social self that is just going through the motions, while the "real" me is wasting away unrecognized.

In contrast to Ch'ien's horizontal self, we might say this is a *vertical* model of the self: the true self is deep inside, covered over by layers of inauthenticity and compromise. In the psychoanalytic world, the horizontal model corresponds to Philip Bromberg's model of dissociation; the vertical model is represented by Freud's theory of repression and D. W. Winnicott's theory of a false self of social accommodation and conventionality overlaying our true feelings and aspirations. Faced with these two models, I suggest we take a horizontal perspective—that is, we place them side by side rather than decide one needs to take priority over the other.

In some circumstances, we can make good use of the notion of a real, inner me that needs to be acknowledged in order to flourish. Coming to terms with one's sexual identity might be one such example; giving oneself free rein to develop an artistic impulse might be another. But in other circumstances, the horizontal model makes more psychological sense. We need love and we need work. Both needs are genuine and neither is deeper or more the real me than the other. Even though we may experience very real, painful conflicts between the two, we cannot resolve that conflict by wholly choosing one over the other.

We can't let either side win exclusive title to "the real me." Perhaps, like the three ancient witches of Greek mythology who have a single eye that they pass between them, we will have to learn to pass our "I" back and forth between a whole of crowd of "me's," no one of which is entitled to hold on to it indefinitely.

CHAPTER TEN

FACING IMPERMANENCE

SUN-FACED BUDDHA, MOON-FACED BUDDHA

Great Master Ma-tsu (Jap. Baso) was sick.
The temple superintendent asked him: "Teacher, how is your venerable health these days?"
The great master said: "Sun-faced Buddha; Moon-faced Buddha."

Mary Beard has remarked that every generation of classicists laments that the knowledge of Latin and Greek is rapidly slipping away in the hands of the younger generation. Yet each generation has in turn been looked back upon by the next as a "golden age" of classical scholarship. Something is going on, she argued, that goes beyond any measurable change in the level of classical education or expertise, something that reflects the nature of the study of the classics themselves. From a psychoanalytic perspective, one might say that the classicists who lament the decline of their field are enacting something basic about its very nature, namely that the study of the classics is the study of loss.

It is as if the field itself were caught in some kind of identificatory repetition compulsion, forever reenacting the experience of its own decline and fall, of the barbarians at the gates, of the possibility of everything it holds dear being utterly swept away. We study the history of the Greeks and Romans knowing how much of their literature has irrevocably been lost—for instance, of the 123 plays said to have been written by Sophocles, only seven survive. We study a civilization that having once been a seemingly everlasting and invincible empire was swept away so thoroughly that its most famous texts were unavailable for nearly a thousand years, until rediscovered and revived in the Renaissance.

Within the field of classics, the mastery of the Latin and Greek languages serve as the bulwark against loss. It is what we, through our own efforts, can do to preserve the field against the ravages of time. Yet each generation of classicists, according to Beard, fears that fewer and fewer young students are developing the necessary expertise to preserve what the previous generation had labored to uphold. Each generation reenacts the drama of loss, of trying to hold back the tide.

Zen Buddhism has at its core the truth of impermanence, and it too enacts a dialectical drama between the forces of change and the stability of tradition. Zen may be unique in providing a form of meditation practice, zazen, that has remained unchanged for over a thousand years, through which to study impermanence.

In addition, Chinese and Japanese Zen culturally have been pre-occupied with the notion of an unbroken lineage and the unity of realization experience that is said to be unchanged across millennia. If you experience realization, says Master Wu-men, "you will see through the same eyes of the old masters, your eyebrows entangled with theirs." We simultaneously affirm that everything changes, and also that the realization of that truth is an unchanging part of our practice and tradition. The unity of realization experience has been put forth by teachers such as John Daido Loori as a way to simultaneously acknowledge the increasingly unavoidable historical evidence that the traditional lineage charts contain fabrications used to paper over gaps or discontinuities in the lineages and to maintain that those gaps are insignificant in light of the transmission of authentic and presumably identical experience across generations.

The koan curriculum itself is both the manifestation and the perpetuator of the program of experiential continuity. Studying the stories of and by our ancestors, we enter into their lives, become a part of an unbroken chain of practice, and experience for ourselves what they experienced long ago. This requires us to maintain that the cultural and historical differences between twenty-first-century America and, say, eighth-century China can, at the very least, be totally dissolved at the level of the Absolute, the level of the immediacy of "just this."

Koans, of course, do not just reveal the level of the Absolute but progress through an ever more subtle interplay of the relative and the Absolute. Yet what experience, no matter how basic, how primal, can we say is literally the same for us as for our Chinese forebears? Rinzai yelled and hit his monks as a way to present an immediacy freed from any conceptual framework whatsoever, but unquestionably my students would not respond to being hit the way his reportedly did. (Besides, my malpractice insurance wouldn't cover it . . .) Even dying, which one might argue is the one experience that all humans share, cannot be extracted from its cultural surround. In fact, one might argue that much of our cultural surround exists precisely to frame, give meaning to, and transform our experience of dying. Dying in a world in which one anticipates "reincarnation" or in one that is merely the gateway to another world of judgment and eternal reward or punishment is not the same experience as dying in a world in which death is final and no afterlife is to be counted on or dreaded.

What does it say about Zen that it is preoccupied with its own continuity and the unchanging nature of realization? In some way parallel to the classicists who are engaged in preserving the literature of dead languages, while lamenting their own impending professional decline, Zen Buddhists teach the unavoidable nature of change while doing everything they can to ensure that the teaching and the teacher's descendants continue practicing in the same way and with the same koans as they have done for hundreds of years. Having had the chance to meet and talk with dozens of Zen teachers over the years, I can think of only one who told me she gave no thought to having a Dharma heir and that when it came time for her to retire, she would simply close the doors to the zendo and that would be that. One needn't believe that the continuation of the Dharma depends on the continuation of *my* Dharma, *my* lineage. The Dharma simply describes the way the world is: impermanent and interconnected. That reality has been and will be there to discover long before and long after there are no longer people who call themselves "Buddhists."

In one way, the koan about Great Master Ma-tsu with which we opened this chapter couldn't be more straightforward. In another, it goes against the grain of everything we do in our ordinary lives. The Sun-faced Buddha is said to live for 1,800 years, the Moon-faced Buddha for a single day. Both are buddhas, both perfect and complete in themselves. Health is a part of our lives; sickness is a part of our lives. Birth is part of all our lives; death is part of all our lives. We say the words, we know the facts, and yet . . . Most of us can barely deal with changes in the weather; who among us can deal with serious changes in our health? Fortunately we get lots of practice with each and will only get more.

Our preoccupation with continuity plays out at every level. It plays out at the level of our mood, moment to moment. Are we able to remain sunny all the time, in all circumstances? Should we be? Could the koan be: Sunny Buddha, grouchy Buddha? Master Ma-tsu allows the ups and downs of his health to be of no concern; should we be able to say the same thing about our mood, or would that be some kind of failure to maintain equanimity? Is equanimity a state, or is it a tolerance for the free flow of states from one into another? That's the basic dilemma we are presented with here, reduced to a question about states of health.

As with our health, our entire lives, our families' lives, our lineages, our traditions, our country, our species, our planet, all are subject to change and eventual extinction. We look at the fossil record and see that vast extinctions repeatedly occurred throughout earth's history. Who can doubt that humankind will not one day be part of that record? Dinosaur Buddha? Dodo Buddha? Human Buddha? In the great sweep of evolutionary time, are we human beings sun-faced buddhas or moon-faced buddhas?

We presume that humans are the only animals that know they are going to die and the only animals that build monuments, leave heirs and legacies, carve their names in stone, or have buildings named after them when they die. We acknowledge our mortality with one hand, only to create fantasies of immortality, life after death, eternal souls, and reincarnation with the other. Perhaps even Buddhists can stand only so much impermanence.

Master Ma-tsu says to us: let come what will come; let go what will go. Very simple. Next to impossible. That impossibility, too, must be one of the attributes of Buddha.

CHAPTER ELEVEN

DESIRE & ATTACHMENT

THE OLD WOMAN, THE HERMIT, AND THE YOUNG GIRL

There was an old woman who supported a hermit. For twenty years she always had a girl, sixteen or seventeen years old, take the hermit his food and wait on him.

One day, she told the girl to give the monk a close hug and ask, "What do you feel just now?"

The hermit responded,

"A old tree on a cold cliff;

Midwinter no warmth."

The girl went back and told this to the old woman. The woman said, "For twenty years I've supported this vulgar good-for-nothing!" So saying, she drove the monk out and burned down the hermitage.

Even though one of the central tenets of Buddha's teaching was interdependence, one rarely hears this interpreted in terms of *emotional* interdependence. How can we link up, in our own thought and practice, the rather abstract idea that we are inseparably entwined with the world in a nexus of causal, karmic relations, with the more immediate experience of being emotionally tied to our family, our loved ones, our peers, friends, and an ever-expanding social network of relations? When we speak abstractly about causal relations, we realize that not only is this net inescapable but that who we are is the sum of our relations within the net. Yet when we speak of emotional connections, we all too often switch into a language of entanglements, clinging, attachment, and dependency, as if all of these ways of being connected, unlike our more neutral sounding causal relations, were somehow extraneous, superfluous, or obstacles to realizing our true nature. Where emotional connections are concerned, Zen all too easily slips into the language of autonomy, self-reliance, and independence, somehow denying that our interdependence inevitably exists at this personal level as well.

Even my old teacher Joko Beck, who perhaps more than any other single figure in contemporary American Zen brought an awareness of emotional reality into Zen practice, was reluctant to engage with feelings such as dependency, vulnerability, love, and attachment as other than obstacles encountered on the way. She rightly noted that "love is a word not often mentioned in Buddhist texts," but she approached that lack like a doctor dismayed to find that his patients were all suffering from a disease that had never been mentioned in medical school. Quoting the Soto master Menzan Zenji (1683–1769), she said it was not enough to cut off delusive *thought*, one must melt away the root of *emotion-thought*—by which Menzan meant our emotional attachment to our particular self-centered thoughts and expectations—otherwise, these same thoughts will arise over and over again, like a weed that has not been cut away at its very root. And romantic love, she said, was where "emotion-thought gets really out of hand." This is *Romeo and Juliet*, absent all the poetry, presented as a cautionary tale of teen suicide.

Joko's great achievement was to show us how to work with anger, anxiety, and avoidance in our practice; all the emotional signposts of our saying "no" to some aspect of this moment's experience. Whatever part of ourselves we want to call "not me," whatever aspect of the other that is not meeting our expectations, *that* is what she taught us to embrace in our sitting. For Joko, relationships were a great field for practice because they inescapably illuminated our self-image, how we saw ourselves and how we wanted to be seen and treated by others. They revealed all the ways we employed others in our curative fantasies, imagining that what was missing in ourselves could be supplied by another, and so on. She wrote that for most people, relationships came down to the desire for pleasure and using the other as a source of that pleasure. She goes on to say:

> This relationship is there, out there, and it's supposed to give me pleasure. At the very least, it shouldn't give me discomfort. In other words, we make this relationship into a dish of ice cream. That dish of ice cream is there to give me pleasure and give me comfort. That very few of us view our relationship in any other light . . .

Although I don't want to reduce her teaching on the subject of love to this single metaphor, it is significant to me that she chose something like ice cream as a stand-in for what most of us want and get out of relationships. It is nothing we actually need, nothing that is essential to life, merely something sweet, not very nutritious, and actually probably bad for our health. Go ahead and have a little if you must, but watch out . . .

In the chapter of *Everyday Zen* she famously entitled "Relationships Don't Work," she maintained that any expectation whatsoever we might have of our partners was simply part of our self-centered dream. The only love that was genuine was a love that was totally selfless. To truly love somebody "means you give them everything and expect nothing. 'If you need something, I'll give it to you.' Love expects nothing."

This is, to say the least, a strange form of love, in that there is nothing mutual or reciprocal about it. It is a love that we might imagine a mother having for a newborn, but even there so much of the mother-child bond is sustained by the infant's returning the mother's loving gaze, looking up at her with wonder and delight, a partner from the very first days of life in the dance of intersubjectivity. There is an absoluteness in Joko's definition of love that brings to mind the ethical writings of Emannuel Levinas, who declares that our moral obligation to the Other is infinite. And as in Levinas, there is no reciprocity; I cannot hold the Other to be equally responsible to me as I am to him; I must give my love wholly and unconditionally, whether it is returned or not.

Although Joko's picture of love may represent an ideal of selflessness, the problem is how we handle ourselves and others in the less-than-ideal day-to-day reality of our lives. It's like the student who, hearing his teacher declare zazen means to totally die on your cushion, asks if there are any intermediate steps . . .

It's also a model for true love that can go terribly wrong. Attempting to be devoted wholly to the other will almost always (or let me say: *always*, in every case I've ever personally encountered) entail denying or repressing or otherwise splitting off some aspect of one's own genuine needs for love, connection, and reciprocity. I suspect that Joko's personal life story brought her to a place where she said, in effect, "I'm never going to rely on anybody like that again." This personal history included marriage to a dangerously mentally ill husband and working with, in the case of Maezumi Roshi, a Zen teacher whose alcoholism and sexual misconduct devastated the Zen Center of Los Angeles during her years there. Love, and practice, meant giving your all, but expecting—needing—nothing in return. Interdependence was not allowed to mean interdependency. For Joko, relationships were a great vehicle for practice, but not the locus of any genuine emotional need for love or connection.

Although it is only my own personal impression, Joko in her final years was deeply shaken by her increasing physical frailty and dependence on her two Dharma heirs, Elizabeth Hamilton and Ezra Bayda, who lived with and cared for her during her last years at the Zen Center of San Diego. She had always prided herself in her physical fitness, and it was a shock to see her need help to cross the room. At the same time, this teacher who had never wanted to clone herself, who had insisted each of her successors find his or her own voice and direction, became increasingly concerned that her closest heirs were now somehow undermining her teaching.

The last time I saw her, after she moved to Prescott, Arizona, to live with her daughter, and after having, without warning, taken the unprecedented step of trying to revoke the Dharma transmission she had bestowed on Elizabeth and Ezra, she told me how strong she was, how none of her heirs had the power she had, and that giving any of us transmission had probably been a mistake. She spoke of Soen Roshi, not Maezumi, as her true teacher. Anyone who tried to question her version of events was simply a liar, and she knew the truth. I tell this story with great sadness, because it was a moment in which I realized that the person I had learned so much from, on whom I had relied in so many ways for so many years, was no longer present. It was a final lesson in transience, a lesson that no one can promise to stay strong and clear-minded forever, no matter what his or her level of past realization.

In practice, we must confront not just the problems that arise *from* desire, which is the core of the Buddha's teaching, but also the obstacles *to* emotionally necessary and healthy desire that may be the core psychoanalytic teaching. What may look like contentment or acceptance may be a cover for resignation, an unwillingness to feel deeply or take interpersonal risks. Burying our longings and not facing up to a fear of rejection should not be part of a legitimate spiritual solution to the problem of desire. Spending a lifetime trying to actualize a curative fantasy of autonomy should not be allowed to masquerade as the Buddha Way.

Ezra Pound wrote a parody of A. E. Housman that could equally serve as a parody of a certain type of Buddhist view of life. Housman was a classicist and closeted gay man whose unrequited love for a heterosexual college chum fueled his poetry of loss and elegy, most famously in his book *A Shropshire Lad*. The opening stanzas of Pound's *Song in the Manner of Housman* go:

> O woe, woe,
> People are born and die,
> We also shall be dead pretty soon
> Therefore let us act as if we were
> dead already.
>
> The bird sits on the hawthorn tree
> But he dies also, presently.
> Some lads get hung, and some get shot.
> Woeful is this human lot.
> Woe! woe, etcetera . . .

You might say this expresses "life is suffering," while leaving out the part about enlightenment. It also expresses something about the hopelessness of desire and presents as a solution resignation and renunciation, acting "as if we were dead already." While no one would (I hope) consciously advocate such a response to life's disappointments, there is a unmistakable tendency within Buddhist practice to aspire to a condition of imperviousness, an immersion in emptiness that will leave us invulnerable—if not insensate.

This temptation has long been recognized, as the popularity of the koan of "An Old Woman Burns Down a Hermitage" testifies. Although it is not included in any of the traditional koan collections, as one of the only koans to directly address sexuality, it has had a unique and persistent place in koan commentary.

It is strange practice indeed that aspires to the condition of a withered tree, impervious to the conditions, even at the price of lifelessness. Yet all of us seem to harbor some version of this wish that practice make us invulnerable. What is striking here is how the hermit wishes in particular to be invulnerable to any form of sexual desire. It is not enough that he has (presumably) taken a vow of chastity and would never act on his desires; his aspirations go beyond self-control to having no desires at all *to* control. Indeed, he claims to have reached a state where desire cannot even arise.

Like many of our curative fantasies, what is sad here is not that his aspiration is impossible but that it is *almost* possible. We can, after years of practice, make ourselves tough and unfeeling, almost if not entirely unresponsive to simple human emotion. And what have we gained? We must have been terrified by our own minds, our own feelings, our own vulnerability, to want to so thoroughly extirpate this part of ourselves. And so we have created for ourselves a practice in which we have learned to master extremes of physical pain and hardship, while never facing the risks that arise from tenderness, longing, or being in love.

The old woman in this story will have none of the hermit's bogus spirituality. She would have done better to have had a stone statue of the Buddha in her garden all these years. She drives him out, teaching both him and us a lesson.

Yet it's a hard lesson to learn. Especially in the light of all the sexual scandals in twentieth-century American Zen, we can imagine even worse outcomes out there in the hermitage to the young girl's test. For too many of our generation, owning our sexual feelings has meant indulging them in behaviors that, if not actually abusive, were at times reckless and foolish. The third grave precept of Zen admonishes us not to abuse sexuality, and we can see that the hermit in his own way has abused it no less than our errant, sexually permissive peers. Where do we find the Middle Way here? It is the same Middle Way I want to find between Joko's picture of a totally selfless love that expects nothing in return and the love that causes us to do anything, put up with anything, in order to hold on to our love object.

As Thomas Merton—the Trappist monk, who after decades of monastic celibacy found himself falling passionately in love with a young nurse—finally admitted, there can be no real love without attachment, no feeling without vulnerability, and in the end no humanity without reciprocal need. The monk, whether the hermit or the famous Trappist, had better be willing to make a fool of himself. Trying to be a lifeless tree perched on a rocky cliff, come to think of it, is already pretty foolish. In the end, we can and should control our behavior—but not our feelings, and maybe, if you're a monk, not even your blushing at the advances, real or feigned, of a pretty girl. Love may make fools of us all, and it should. It is part of the ride down the stream of samsara, and we might as well enjoy the ride. We should know it's going to be rocky, and we shouldn't be surprised if we get hurt.

If we are not going to banish attachment, desire, and dependency from our lives, how should we understand and practice with them? From a psychoanalytic perspective, love and relationships are as necessary as oxygen in our life.

As Heinz Kohut said:

> Values of independence are phony, really. There is no such thing. There can be no pride in living without oxygen. We're not made that way. It is nonsense to try to give up symbiosis and become an independent self. An independent self is one that is clever enough to find a good selfobject support system and stay in tune with its needs

and the changing of generations. To that system one must be willing to give a great deal.

We are often confused about the role others play in maintaining what we think of as our own stable sense of who we are, our equanimity or what we misconstrue as our autonomous capacity for self-control. Kohut used the term *selfobject* to denote the way the self's identity and (seemingly) individual capacities are intimately and inextricably tied to, and are dependent on, others (or *objects* in psychoanalytic jargon). Kohut purposely did not hyphenate the term *selfobject* to emphasize that there was no gap between self and Other when seen from this perspective of codependent functioning.

A interesting colloquial example of a selfobject occurs in the expression "to get someone's goat." For a long time, I never thought about what this literally meant and imagined that someone's "goat" was just a slang expression for that part of a person that is overly sensitive or reactive. But the expression has a very specific origin. Apparently, the presence of goat can have a very soothing effect on a temperamental thoroughbred racehorse, and goats were kept in the horses' stalls to keep the animals calm. Unscrupulous rivals of the horse's owner, however, were prone to stealing the goat, thereby destabilizing the horse before a big race. Thus "getting someone's goat" means literally depriving someone of who or what they need to stay calm or regulated. And that something is actually outside, not inside, though we feel the effect of its loss as if something *inside* of us were now missing. As Kohut implied, how we feel about ourselves, and how well or badly we function, may depend on to whom we are attached and how secure that attachment feels. It is perhaps worth reviewing something of the psychoanalytic literature on attachment, especially as it has grown out of infant research, and see how that word is used in a fundamentally different way than we find in Buddhism.

Freud's original theory saw people motivated by unconscious sexual and aggressive wishes. As individuals, we struggle to regulate and control our impulses and bring them in line with the outside demands of reality and the rules of society. The evolution of psychoanalytic theory beyond Freud's original formulation was propelled by an increasing awareness that we were not simply pleasure-seekers but people seekers—that a need for other people was a primary motivation in its own right and not simply a byproduct of more basic biological needs for food and sex. This turn in psychoanalysis was called *object relations* (*object* being the technical word unfortunately chosen to refer to other people) and is associated with the work of Ronald Fairbairn and D. W. Winnicott. It also formed the basis for a new psychological study of infants and children, pioneered by John Bowlby. Whereas Freud had oriented his psychoanalytic inquiries into the fantasy life of children, Bowlby stressed the actual family environment and particularly the role of separation from the mother during the early years of childhood. Bowlby studied the effects on children of being separated from their mother during hospitalization and other disruptions of normal family life. His work was experimentally extended by Mary Ainsworth, who developed a protocol for studying patterns of separation and reunion between children and parents that provided the foundation for what has become known as attachment theory.

Ainsworth's experiment involved observing the reactions of one-year-old babies throughout a series of scenarios during which they were first in a room with their mother and toys; then in the room with the mother and with a stranger also present; with the stranger while the mother leaves the room; alone with both the mother and stranger absent; and finally when the mother returns to the baby. Although the babies at first displayed predictable responses of distress at being left with a stranger or being left alone, what

Ainsworth discovered was that there were clearly different categories of response in the final *reunion* with the mother.

One group of babies, having become distressed and crying on being left alone, responded to the mother's return with increased, attention-getting crying and made moves to be picked up. Once picked up, they were very responsive and soothe-able and stopped crying, often within fifteen seconds. This was the group that became known as *securely attached*. A second group of babies, who seemed to respond to being left alone with added degrees of distress, reacted to the mother's return by seeming to be pulled in two directions at once. Although they immediately sought contact, they squirmed and kicked when picked up and were very difficult to soothe. Their inconsolability might persist for several minutes in sharp contrast to the securely attached babies quieting down in a few seconds. This group was called *ambivalently attached*. The third style of response was in some ways stranger, subtler, and more unexpected than the first two. These babies appeared less distressed than the other babies at the mother's leaving, more preoccupied with their toys, more content to be left with a stranger. Though they cried at the mother's leaving and wanted to be picked up by her on her return, they seemed distracted, not making eye contact, turning away from the mother's face back to their toys. These babies readily return to quiet play while ignoring the mother. The initial impression made by this type of baby was that they were "dream babies"—independent and unperturbed. But in fact, they were what Ainsworth called *avoidant*, babies who seemingly became indifferent in response to separation as a way of mitigating the distress of the disruption. Psychologists had to be carefully trained to be attuned to the differences in reunion behaviors.

It turned out, according to Ainsworth, that it was particularly "difficult to recognize the avoidant response, partly because the avoidant children often look so good—independent, engageable, emotionally robust—that an observer might tend to rationalize or overlook the peculiarities of their reunion behavior." Although these attachment styles were originally studied in one-year-olds, subsequent research identified the ways these patterns developed and persistent later in childhood and even into adulthood. Nor did these patterns of attachment simply reflect different temperaments in the children; they corresponded to different patterns of parenting, especially by their mothers.

For example, looking at the mothers of two-year-olds just entering a developmental phase in which they increasingly practice independent play, researchers found significant differences among how the mothers responded to their children's experiments in independence. Mothers of securely attached toddlers knew how to be a secure presence to their children, neither excessively withdrawing or impinging. The mothers of the ambivalently attached children, on the other hand, never could seem to maintain an appropriate distance. Some swooped in at the first signs of the child's distress, seemingly unable themselves to tolerate the child's frustration in any new situation. Others remained passively distant and never knew when their child actually could use a little help or a push to try something new. Their children often gave up quickly whenever a new toy or task wasn't immediately satisfying.

Although there are not conclusive longitudinal studies showing the progression of different attachment styles all the way into adulthood, for our purposes it is interesting to note some particular features of the ambivalently and dismissively attached children as they grow up. Unlike the securely attached children who easily form friendships and are comfortable with their own feelings and needs, ambivalently attached children often have trouble functioning in groups, yet dread isolation and abandonment. They may be clingy with teachers and often elicit indulgent and infantilizing responses in return. The dismissively attached child may grow up having few friends and having difficulty in groups. As adults they may be dismissive of the importance of love and connection and valorize independence and autonomy.

What I would like us to take away from these attachment studies is the way the different styles may play out in Buddhist practice settings and how practice itself can collude with many defensive features of the insecurely attached individual. I remember my reaction upon first coming across the description of avoidant babies—those who seemed to be the most independent of their mothers, the least disrupted by her absence, the most seemingly self-sufficient, if not all that easily held or responsive: "What good little Buddhists!"

We need to understand the ways our forms of practice, especially in community settings, attracts and responds to different types of individuals. The ambivalently attached type who is needy and idealizing of the teacher, endlessly loyal out of fear of rejection, a perpetual, infantilized student who never can, or wants to, grow up. The dismissive student—or teacher—who underplays the need for any personal relationships at all, for whom practice is everything, for whom transcending vulnerability and the need for personal love is not seen as a problem but a spiritual solution. Ambivalently or dismissive attached people—and most of us have some aspect of these qualities—above all else need to find relationships and settings in which they can gradually become securely attached in ways they never have been before.

Traditional monastic training centers may offer the security of great stability and predictability in their daily routine, but may be dismissive of students' need for personal attention or understanding. Teachers may actually foster chronic insecurity by claiming that any need for predictability, reliability, or responsiveness is nothing but "egoistic attachment," which must be treated by being continually thwarted. Such teachers may appear to foster what appears to be great personal devotion from their students but which is, in fact, a form of desperate clinging.

The less we are given secure personal love and understanding, the more we will cling to idealized, distant, but tantalizing parental figures. Teachers themselves may be unaware of the extent to which they are fostering the dependent behaviors they say they are trying to undo in their students. Constantly pulling the emotional rug out from under students, keeping them off balance or unsure of their place in the community or in the teacher's regard, may be rationalized as a way to free them from their ego, but all too often will simply make the insecure more insecure and the dismissive even more so. The teacher, herself, may be engaging in a form of dissociation. Dismissive of her own emotional needs, she projects them onto her student, who is seen as embodying all the split-off disowned aspects of the teacher's own dependent, needy self. The teacher's response to the student's need for security and attachment may then take on a sadistic quality, as she attacks (in the name of practice) in the student those aspects of herself that are an ongoing, if unconscious, source of shame and self-hatred.

How do the teacher's own split-off needs for attachment get gratified? One unfortunate, if recurring, outcome is the teacher becoming inappropriately emotionally or sexually involved with a student. Thomas Merton's suddenly falling in love with a student nurse when he was hospitalized in his fifties is a classic case of an unacknowledged longing for personal love erupting in the midst of a life devoted to a disembodied, transcendent love of God. Most cases of teachers' romantic involvement with students probably arise from this kind of unconscious need suddenly breaking through a longstanding shell of dismissiveness and detachment.

While there are undoubtedly examples of teachers who have been serial sexual predators, I believe the majority of cases have resulted from the teacher's healthy but hitherto split off need for attachment finally being acted out. There have been numerous cases of teachers marrying their students, which in some ways is an attempt to legitimize what would otherwise threaten to be an illicit liaison. However, as is the case of therapists marrying their patients, there often remains an unresolved transferential and countertransferential shadow hanging over the relationship. How clear can either party really have been about their respective needs for dominance or submission, to be entitled to what is forbidden to others, to be or to capture an elusive and illicit love object?

The situation is even more problematic when the teacher gives Dharma transmission to his student/partner. Outside observers can't help but wonder at the legitimacy of such transmissions and to question how objective or rigorous any teacher can be when training their lover. Yet spousal transmission is increasingly becoming normalized in American Zen, with some lineages like White Plum seeming to almost make a specialty of it. Maezumi Roshi's main successors, Bernie Glassman, Daido Loori, Genpo Merzel, and Chozen Bays, all have given Dharma transmission to their partners or lovers—with Bernie Roshi holding what is probably some sort of record by having giving transmission to all three of his wives.

Yet in the context of a tradition that has been dismissive of emotional attachment, perhaps the integration of love and practice is not to be derided (even though as a psychoanalyst, I admit that I harbor qualms that it feels too analogous to marrying one's patient). We need to evolve forms and ways of talking that legitimize personal needs, sexual as well as dependent, as Zen increasingly moves into lay life, and out of a morality based on monastic conduct that seems increasingly less and less relevant.

Is there any place in traditional Zen from which to launch a legitimization of emotional needs and ties? There seems little there to build upon, except the father/son–like ties between master and disciple.

The stories of the old Chinese masters include many such examples of filial devotion between student and teacher. Chao-chou, long after his own realization, stayed by his master Nan-ch'uan's side for another forty years until the old man passed away. These home-leaving monks naturally transferred their need for personal connection onto the teacher. Zen Buddhism, as presented in the lineage, has been the model of a family business, handed down one generation after another from surrogate father to surrogate son.

In Japan, transmission and the handing down of the abbotship of a temple often became literally a father to son affair. In our own day, following the disruptions in Shunryu Suzuki's lineage caused by scandals at the San Francisco Zen Center, the lineage's symbolic integrity was restored by Mel Weitsman going to Japan to formally receive Dharma transmission from Suzuki Roshi's son Hoitsu, who, while he inherited his father's temple, never had a teaching relationship with the Americans who now became his father's Dharma "heirs."

This filial sense, as embodied in a preoccupation with lineage, is one of the few directions from which personal affection and connection can be legitimately smuggled into the austerities of Zen training. We need to find more ways and forms of acknowledging the legitimacy of attachment needs in our practice. They will always be there, and given all the difficulties that have arisen in the personal lives of contemporary students and teachers, there is no longer any more room under the rug for anything to be swept.

CHAPTER TWELVE

MUTUAL RECOGNITION

YÜN-MEN'S MEDICINE AND DISEASE

Yün-men (Jap. Unmon) said, "Medicine and disease quell each other. The whole world is medicine. What is your self?"

One strand of Western philosophy, exemplified by Descartes, grounds our sense of self on the absolute reality of our inner experience. The only thing I can be sure that exists is the thinking self that is investigating its own existence. Our knowledge of other people and of the world itself is secondary. The question for philosophy then becomes how does this fundamentally *inner* self connect to and gain knowledge of the world? How reliable can that knowledge be? How can we ever be sure that we actually know what is going on outside of our inner subjective world, that other people exist, or if they do, that their experience is in any reliable way commensurable with our own?

This way of thinking gives rise to what philosophers call the problem of *intentionality*, which has a technical philosophical sense of *aboutness*. How can words and concepts reliably hook on to things in the world? If one starts, as Descartes did, with the idea of an isolated mind attempting to prove its own existence and the

existence of other minds and an outer world, one is almost automatically condemned to an inescapable existential alienation from
what Buddhism calls our essential interconnectedness. This position
has, from the psychoanalytic perspective of intersubjectivity, been
called the *myth of the isolated mind*.

Robert Stolorow and George Atwood (who significantly always
coauthored their papers) outlined three main areas of alienation
from our natural embeddedness in all life. First, alienation from
nature, including the illusion that "there is a sphere of inner freedom from the constraints of animal existence and mortality." Second, alienation from social life, including the illusion that "each
individual knows only his own consciousness and thus is forever
barred from direct access to experiences belonging to other people . . . which ignores the constitutive role of relationship to the
other in a person's having any experience at all." And third, alienation from subjectivity itself, so that the contents of the mind are
reified so as to appear to possess the properties of material things
of the outer world (e.g., as psychic structures with "localization,
extension, enduring substantiality") and that the mind itself constitutes a kind of inner space from which we look out, as through
a window, at the outer world.

Thomas Kuhn, the renowned philosopher of science, who coined
the notion of paradigm shifts as a model for scientific revolution,
claimed that the systems of thought before and after a paradigm
shift were incommensurable. That is to say, scientists after the shift
lived in a different world than their predecessors. For instance, if
someone believes that the earth is the immovable center of the universe, and they are told that no, in fact the earth revolves around
the sun, they are not simply receiving an isolated new bit of scientific information, their whole world is undergoing a change. The
meaning of the word "earth" itself is no longer the same.

Errol Morris, now widely known as a documentary filmmaker,
was once a student of Kuhn's in philosophy. He recalls arguing with

his mentor about this whole notion of incommensurability and Kuhn's exasperation with his inability to accept his account of paradigm shifts. Supposedly Kuhn's frustration got the better of him and he ended one argument by hurling an ashtray at Morris's head. The dilemma that Morris tirelessly pointed out was that Kuhn, as a historian of science, was in the business of reconstructing the conceptual frameworks of scientists who operated within different paradigms. If these systems were, as he claimed, incommensurable, how could he understand their differences? How could he avoid misinterpreting them in light of his own current paradigm?

The dilemma we face, individually and across cultures, is how is empathy (even translation) possible at all? What do we have to have in common in order to understand one another? Wittgenstein declared, "If a lion could talk, we would not understand him"— because we do not share a commensurable form of life in which to ground a common language.

However, when it comes to other people, it may be that our understanding of them is as certain as anything can be. "Am I less certain that this man is in pain than twice two is four?" asked Wittgenstein.

Wittgenstein and, in his own very different way, Hegel asserted that our knowledge of our self and of the world must begin in the opposite direction from Descartes' starting point; not from the inside out, but outside in. Seen from this perspective, the problem of isolated minds and the dilemma of intentionality dissolves. For Wittgenstein, the whole of our seemingly internal subjective experience is embedded in language, and it is our embeddedness in a shared human form of life that gives us a simultaneous purchase of inner and outer reality. Wittgenstein famously asserted there could be no such thing as a *private* language, a language of solipsistic inner experience unconnected in its origins to any other speaker or shared form of life. Most fundamentally he asked, how would someone ever *learn* it?

Hegel, in a way that prefigured the development of relational psychoanalysis, spoke of an emerging self attempting to experience itself as a center of absolute agency but being able to do so only by means of having an *impact* on another, and by gaining the *recognition* of the other of its own existence. Unlike the self in Descartes who pulls himself up unassisted by his own logical bootstraps, the self in Hegel is created by the ongoing dialectic or interplay of self and other. Psychoanalyst Jessica Benjamin took Hegel's abstract account of the development of the self and connected it to the emerging research on mother-infant interaction.

Rather than start with an adult philosopher sitting alone in a room asking himself the rather peculiar question of whether he exists or not, Benjamin looked at how babies actually develop a sense of self through interaction with the mother. In her account, we learn the existence of our own mind at the very same time we learn of the existence of other minds. I, the baby, am the one who makes Mommy smile, and Mommy is the one who makes me smile. In other words, Benjamin's Hegelian baby simultaneously develops a sense of her own self in and through her sense of the other, the mother.

For Benjamin, and other relationally oriented analysts, we are not born inside a solipsistic bubble out of which that we must struggle to escape. Neither are we stranded on an island of our own subjectivity, sending words out like messages in a bottle, hoping that they land and somehow connect to a distant world of objects. Broadly speaking, the post-Freudian movements in psychoanalysis, whether they describe themselves as self-psychological, intersubjective, or relational, are positing a post-Cartesian world of interconnection and interdependence. Like their distant philosophical cousins in the lineages of Wittgenstein and Hegel, they see the problem of human relations, not in terms of isolated individuals who need reasons (whether at the level of drives or the social contract) to form family and social connections, but as a chapter in the ongoing evolution of an interpersonal, linguistic, and social network, that we, to the extent that we are human at all, cannot be imagined to in any way preexist. This fundamental co-creation of self and world, of the interlocking nature of inner and outer is, to my mind, beautifully prefigured in Yün-men's declaration about medicine and sickness. There can be no such thing as "medicine" without a corresponding notion of "sickness." Just as the famous Zen poem known as the "Identity of Relative and Absolute" declares that "light and darkness are a pair," we cannot have one without the other. In fact, when Yün-men goes on to ask "What is the self?" we are meant to realize we can't have *anything* without *everything* else. Hakuin's comment on this koan flatly asserts that the self *is* the world.

There is no place outside the self from which to ask what is the self; no place outside the world from which to ask what is the world; no place outside of existence from which to ask whether I or the world exist or not.

If we think only in terms of opposites, like medicine and sickness, when Yün-men declares that the whole world is medicine and then asks "What is the self?" we might be tempted to say that the self is sickness—that the illusion of the "self" is the sickness from which we are trying to recover. But if we split everything into halves, we can only arrive at half-truths. Yün-men challenges us to take life whole.

CHAPTER THIRTEEN

DIFFERENCE

LIU AND KUEI-SHAN

Liu (Jap. Ryutetsema) arrives at Kuei-shan's (Jap. Isan) place, and Kuei-shan said, "Old cow, you've come!" Liu said, "There's a big feast on Mt. Taishan tomorrow, teacher. Are you going?" Kuei-shan lay down. With that Liu left.

Boundaries make us what we are.

Biologists have suggested that the most fundamental requirement of a living organism is the creation of a boundary—something that demarcates inside from outside. In order for any sort of molecular self-replicating chemical processes (which would form the basis of reproduction and evolution) to occur, there must, first of all, be something like a membrane or cell wall that keeps the chemical reactants from simply being washed away in the surrounding primordial soup. Anything that we consider to be alive must, at the most basic level, be engaged in maintaining this basic organizational integrity.

When we go on to speak of the inseparability of any organism from its ecological surround, we must not lose sight of the other side of the equation in which separation is as necessary as integration for life to exist. While our Buddhist practice will traditionally decry the way we all too typically become trapped on the separation side of that equation, many practitioners may become equally trapped in the fantasy of living exclusively on the side of integration and nonseparation. What they neglect or lose sight of is precisely any sense of what is allowed to count for them as a psychologically necessary boundary. Psychological boundaries are as fundamental to what it is to be alive and human as cell membranes. The violation of necessary and appropriate boundaries is the basis of what we mean by incest, assault, and rape.

Beyond the need to ward off actual trauma, at the more ordinary, everyday level we need to maintain a *stimulus barrier*, a psychophysiological mechanism for filtering informational and emotional input, lest we be flooded by both sensory and informational noise. One of the clear benefits of meditation (and medications like Prozac and other SSRIs) is the way it strengthens our stimulus barrier so we are less prone to be frazzled, frustrated, or (at the extremes) reactively provoked by our emotional surround. On another level, a cell wall is literally a *semipermeable membrane*; that is, it regulates what and how much passes from outside to inside and vice versa.

We can regard the psychological (and/or Zen) equivalent of such a membrane as the capacity to let thoughts come and go, without their impinging, sticking, or disrupting our sitting still. When we are psychologically fragile, we may try to protect ourselves by setting up a rigid barrier to keep certain thoughts or feelings at bay. But such barriers are almost always brittle and self-defeating; they lead us to see the outside world in terms of threats of impingement or intrusion and leave us in the position of forever trying to plug leaks in our emotional dykes. An optimally functioning membrane efficiently moves nutrients in and moves wastes out of the cell. Our psychological equivalent likewise lets thoughts and feelings move freely in and out of our minds, not getting stuck in them and not having to ward them off.

An account of human civilization could be written entirely in terms of the transformation of the way we perceive boundaries between ourselves and others. From what we imagine about our prehistoric ancestors living in small, family-centered clusters (or tribes dominated by an alpha male), we could trace our evolution in terms of the organization of the group, be it around direct blood-lines, geography, ethnicity, race, or religion. The formation of any self-identity by definition involves the creation of a boundary, the identification of what's "not-me," an Other. Part of our practice will involve dissolving those boundaries, but another equally important part of practice will involve coming to respect them, and to both acknowledge and accept difference.

In the words of Zen teacher Carolyn Atkinson:

> The practice of acceptance is what we do with our own minds, with the discouragement and the anger and the fatigue and the wanting, the endless longing for things to be different than they are. When we extend this accepting mind to others, extend it into the realm of our endlessly longing for them to be different than they are, we can call this practice love.

I admire the way Atkinson is not afraid to bring the word "love" into Zen practice. We don't struggle to "be compassionate" to our spouse or our children; we struggle with what it means to *love* someone who so repeatedly hurts, disappoints, and misunderstands us.

My partner once gave me as a present a cartoon drawn by the artist Susan Miller. It shows a scowling, pointy headed, scruffily bearded man with his arms folded across his chest, saying, "Why can't you be more like me?" I have it displayed on a table over which hangs a scroll depicting another scowling old man, Bodhidharma, whom it uncannily resembles. Self-righteousness, often masquerad-ing as Zen practice or as "compassionate" teaching, is the antithesis of love. It demands an elimination of difference and pursues a uniformity of opinion, desire, and taste.

A fantasy of twinship, thought Heinz Kohut, is one form identificatory love can take in childhood when I want to be just like Mommy or Daddy and dress up in their big shoes and shirts. But too often as adults we confuse love with a Procrustean version of twinship, where the other is expected to either diminish or stretch themselves in some painful way to accommodate themselves to our picture of how they should look, feel, and behave. When there is difference, what is supposed to give? Am I supposed to change how I like to do things in order to hold on to the one I love? Or should the other do the changing? Such false *either/or* choices are the stuff of koans, the koans of everyday life. And they can't all be solved simply by an appeal to oneness and an elimination of difference.

Difference and *boundary* are not words that we normally value in Buddhism; they tend to stand in for everything we imagine we are supposed to overcome in the name of oneness and nonseparation. But how we handle difference will be one of the hallmarks of our mature practice. We can't eliminate difference and we can't blend opposites into a conflict-free synthesis—or mush. If your idea of a treat is a chocolate ice cream sundae and mine is sushi, we cannot compromise by having sushi with chocolate sauce. Boundaries must be maintained, differences respected, turns taken, acknowledgments made that, at some very important levels, you are *not* me. That is one very important meaning of love.

Consider the koan with which we began this chapter:

> Liu arrives at Kuei-shan's place, and Kuei-shan said, "Old cow, you've come!" Liu said, "There's a big feast on Mt. Tai tomorrow, teacher. Are you going?" Kuei-shan lay down. With that Liu left.

We have here a dialogue between Kuei-shan and one of the few women mentioned by name in the koan collections, Liu, an old student of Kuei-shan's who has now come for a visit.

She is known, in other cases, by her nickname Iron-Grinder Liu, the implication being that she grinds to dust any monk with whom she has Dharma combat. Maybe our equivalent of Iron-Grinder would be something like Old Ball-Buster. She was evidently a very formidable character, and for better or for worse, she illustrates the kind of equality women have been traditionally offered in Zen practice. The teaching and the training is open to women but they prove themselves by being as tough as the men—if not tougher. There is very little of the feminine that comes through in women in these cases. That's a big part of what is changing for the better in our generation of American Zen.

So Liu comes to visit Kuei-shan and he says, "Old cow, you've come!" "Old cow" is the kind of a humorous pejorative that Zen teachers like to throw around, but "cow" apparently also means a female water buffalo, and the water buffalo is the ox of the ox herding pictures, a symbol of enlightenment. So it's also a backhanded form of praise to call her the old cow. Kuei-shan himself is known to have said, "After I die, two hundred years from now, a water buffalo will be born in this valley with the characters *Kuei-shan* on its side. Tell me, will you call that creature Kuei-shan or Water Buffalo?" So Kuei-shan is also identified with the water buffalo and in a certain sense there's a level of identification and familiarity in him tossing this image back and forth. It's this image of the water buffalo and the old cow that's referred to in the preface, "With splendid noses each is endowed with a powerful appearance." Two fine-looking animals.

What's also unusual about this case is that it is a story about play among equals. It's not the usual kind of koan, where a novice student comes to an old master asking a question, and whether he leaves bewildered or enlightened, there remains a great gap between the teacher and the monk. This is a very different kind of dialogue that comes at the end of the lives of two old teachers enjoying themselves together. The little game that they're playing is about coming and going and is there anything to get or not. Kuei-shan makes the first move when he says, "You've come."

When we go someplace we are usually looking for something. Lots of people have come to me from far away in order to practice. I might ask them: What are you lacking? What are you looking for? Don't you know there is nothing to gain? Nothing to get? Don't you realize that just by showing up you are making a terrible mistake? That's the way he's teasing Liu with "You've come." And she immediately shoots back, "There's a big feast on Mt. Taishan tomorrow, are you going to go?"

Now Mt. Taishan is supposedly hundreds if not a thousand miles away from where this is taking place. So she teases him in turn, "Oh there's a great thing happening far away, are you going to be part of it or are you missing it?" She tosses the ball right back, and in response Kuei-shan just lies down on the ground. There's no place to go, I'm right here, any big feast is happening right here right now. And with that Liu leaves. They started their game with "You've come?" and "Are you going?" and they volleyed back and forth with him lying down—he's not going anywhere—which she counters by leaving. There's no winner, no loser here, they are playing out a little game about coming and going; is there anything to get, is there anywhere to go?

The verse that accompanies this koan uses the imagery of battles and Dharma combat: *With a hundred battles' merit, growing old in great peace, being serene, who is to pick at the details of strategy?* They've both been through a hundred battles, a hundred Dharma combats, and neither of them has anything to win or lose anymore. They are growing old in great peace together. *The jeweled whip and golden horse passing the day at leisure.* A great general might ride into battle with a jeweled whip on a golden horse; these combatants dismount to enjoy the bright moon and refreshing breeze.

From a more modern and psychological perspective, we can use this koan to examine how we encounter and engage difference. First there is the difference of student and teacher, and second the difference between man and woman. What we're presented with here are the ways differences both do and do not make a difference, the way they play at coming and going *versus* lying down and staying still. These actions are very different, but in a way it doesn't matter which side one plays on and which side the other plays on. They fully occupy their own role, their own difference, and there is not one to be preferred over the other.

If I just lie down and say everything is right here, it's true, but I might miss out on something else. Joko used to say, "You know how far I would go to meet a visiting Dharma teacher? Maybe across the room." She wanted to emphasize that *life* is the teacher, everything you need to know is right here in your own mind, in your own body, on your own cushion. Don't go running around thinking someone else has got it. "Oh the enlightened master is coming to town, I've got to go hear her." She really made a big point of pooh-poohing all that stuff.

Of course, I traveled three thousand miles many times a year for a decade to hear her talk that way. Somehow, it was a great pleasure to travel all that way in order to play with someone else who knew there is nowhere to go and nothing to get. It's fun to have playmates and sometime you have to travel to meet them. It's part of the pleasure I've gotten over the years from going to Zen teachers' meetings. There's no point, there is nothing to get, but we can enjoy this kind of play together.

One of the recurring themes of this book is how practice engages the different sides of our self. Most koans can be thought of as having two or more characters that represent different aspects of our self. Most Zen dialogues were called Dharma combat and the metaphor of combat is deeply engrained in Zen literature. Often, in the past, teachers talked as if the way to achieve inner peace is to *kill* the ego. It's a very curious mixed metaphor: we have to kill off something in ourselves in order to find peace.

I believe it was Michael Wenger who said, "People are always exhorting you to practice harder, maybe we should try practicing *softer* for a change." The language of killing the ego or Dharma combat, or cutting through, vanquishing desire and attachment, is really the language of inner conflict projected out into the practice and into the student-teacher relationship. So much of what brings us to practice is the fact that we're *already* at war with ourselves, one part is *already* trying to kill off another part.

It is all too easy for that kind of inner conflict to get co-opted by the language of practice and in the name of spirituality we try to kill our needs, kill our attachments, kill our vulnerability, kill our anger, kill our sexuality, kill our desire for love, kill off anything that will make us need other people and be vulnerable to them. It's a great problem when practice is co-opted by those kinds of inner conflict, and yet, it's also the skillful means of the language of Zen that it draws out that language of conflict and puts it into koans where we can really see it and can make it explicit. Then we can see what we've been up to.

We can see that we're always engaged in feeling like there's something wrong with me that I've got to get rid of, or there's something missing I've got to get—the whole fantasy of he's got it and I don't. All these are the sources of inner turmoil and inner self hate that we project out into these old stories and try to wrestle with metaphorically and emotionally. But the real resolution of any of these conflicts is never going to be one side killing off the other. We never kill off anything in ourselves, or at least I hope we don't. The resolution in our practice needs to look a lot more like the resolution in this dialogue where two old practice partners play with their difference, play with the whole idea of coming and going, getting or not getting.

The playful dialogue between Kuei-shan and Liu can illustrate for us both the peaceful resolution of different aspects of the self and the resolution of the conflicts that occur when we encounter real differences in the world, differences like those between men and women, that are not simply erased or dissolved into oneness.

What with all the images of cows and water buffalos in this koan, I find myself thinking of it in terms of a children's book, one with animals as the characters. And I imagined a little children's book about Duck and Bunny.

Bunny is always complaining that Duck just paddles slowly around in his little pond all day and never wants to go anywhere. Duck complains Bunny is always running around and doesn't know how to sit still. Duck is noisy and quacks and quacks; Bunny is very quiet and just nibbles her food. (And she has this rather unpleasant habit of eating her own poop—rabbits are coprophagic after all—but maybe that wouldn't be in a children's book. Never mind . . .) "Why can't you be more like me?" each one says to the other.

And I would imagine this little picture book, with each page showing Duck and Bunny talking about their differences. One is fat and waddles, the other is sleek and fast. One loves the water, the other hates getting wet. But in the end, on the very last page of the book, you would see Duck and Bunny holding hands and the caption would be, Duck and Bunny are friends.

This is the lesson of our koan, as well. Kuei-shan and Liu are friends. They're very different, yet they are also very much the same. Their differences both do and don't make a difference.

Can we look this way at the different halves of ourselves that are so used to being in conflict, the differences that we think make such a big difference? Instead of having one half triumph over the other, instead of having a winner and a loser within ourselves, how about if the two sides were friends?

CHAPTER FOURTEEN

THE LAST WORD

HSUEH-FENG THE RICE COOK

Hsueh-feng (Jap. Seppo) served as cook while at the monastery. One day the meal was late. Tê-shan (Jap. Tokusan) arrived at the Dharma hall holding his bowls. Hsueh-feng remarked, "Old fellow, the gong has not yet rung, the drum has not yet sounded. So where are you going with the bowls?" At that, Tê-shan returned to his quarters. Hsueh-feng told Yen-t'ou (Jap. Ganto) about this. And Yen-t'ou remarked, "As you might expect, Tê-shan does not yet understand the last word."

Hearing of this, Tê-shan called an attendant to summon Yen-t'ou and asked, "Don't you approve of this old monk?" Yen-t'ou whispered his intended meaning, whereupon Tê-shan desisted.

The next day when he went to the Dharma hall to speak, Tê-shan was not the same as usual. Rubbing his hands and laughing, Yen-t'ou cried, "Luckily, the old fellow has understood the last word. From now on, no one under heaven will be able to prevail over him."

This koan starts out as a story about getting things right and getting things wrong. Hsueh-feng is the cook, and the meal is late. Somehow, that doesn't figure in the story, though you'd think it was Hsueh-feng's responsibility to get the food out on time. Instead, it features the old teacher Tê-shan who comes down to the Dharma hall at the usual time for meals. Hsueh-feng says, in effect, "Hey, what are you doing here? The gong hasn't sounded yet." Tê-shan doesn't say a word, he just turns around and goes back to his room. Tê-shan has gotten the time wrong, but it's not hard to see that Hsueh-feng might be doing something wrong in return by criticizing his teacher. We have in our zendo many moments like this. I give my students lots of opportunity to treat me like Tê-shan; I make lots of mistakes. I'm always getting the time wrong and during the week, I can somehow never remember whether it's the night to have a service or not, whether we're going to the altar in the back room or the front room. Someone's always having to correct me, giving my students lots of opportunities just like in this case. I hope by the time I'm Tê-shan's age (he's supposed to be eighty in this story) I respond to corrections with as much grace as he does.

Hsueh-feng has a certain arrogance about him, a sense of being somebody. Being the cook is usually right up there with being the head monk in a monastery, and he's a little proud of his position and at catching his teacher off. His friend Yen-t'ou sees that and does something subtle in response. He doesn't reprove Hsueh-feng for his bad behavior in the way that Hsueh-feng reproved Tê-shan. He doesn't fall into the trap of criticizing him for criticizing. He sets up a little game with Tê-shan for Hsueh-feng's sake. He says to Hsueh-feng, "Tê-shan doesn't understand the last word." He's really setting a little trap for him (and for us). Tê-shan hears about this and calls him in and says, "What are you doing?" and Yen-t'ou whispers something into his ear. Here, the koan is setting another little hook for you, the listener. In dokusan you might be asked,

"What did Yen-t'ou whisper in Tê-shan's ear?" Whatever it was, Tê-shan is silent and just nods. The next day, however, he's different. Yen-t'ou gets up in front of everybody and says, "The old man has finally gotten the last word." Now, we don't hear how Hsueh-feng reacts to this whole little play. We end up standing in for Hsueh-feng; how do *we* react to this little drama, how do we react to the whole idea that the old man didn't have the last word and now gets it? What's the last word? It's a wonderful phrase that Yen-t'ou apparently used a number of times in his teaching. It's a phrase like "original face," one that sends people running off looking in all the wrong places for its meaning.

What do we think of when we hear something like "the last word"? Here, it seems to imply a final insight that would make the old man impeccable—he wouldn't make anymore dumb mistakes like the one he made yesterday. As I said, at one level this kind of story is about what it means to get it right or get it wrong. When we start out practicing it looks like the zendo is full of rules and rituals that are easy to get wrong, and we think that our task as students is to learn to get them right. But the deeper lesson is how to get them wrong, how to be able to get them wrong in the manner of Tê-shan. If we think that the way to avoid Hsueh-feng's criticism is to never make a mistake, we end up endlessly judgmental and critical. Every zendo I've been in seems to contain a person who is the house scold; someone who has been around awhile and who thinks he or she has it right and that it is his or her job to remind everyone else what the right way is. For the rest of us, the challenge is to respond to scolding by not reciprocating it, to meet a scowl with a smile.

Another way to understand a koan like this is to try to identify in turn with each of the characters, the way we try to understand a dream by seeing each part of the dream as an aspect of ourselves.

Tê-shan can represent the wise part of ourselves, the part that feels stable and centered in what we are doing. After we've practiced even a little while, we may develop some feeling for that. Yet there's always this other part, the Hsueh-feng part, that keeps nagging at us, "You're not doing it right." He says that even to Tê-shan. All of us have an inner voice that, once in a while, or maybe a lot of the time, tells us, "You're not doing it right." Here it's done relatively playfully. There's a little one-up-manship involved, but there's none of the real nastiness that we tend to bring to the part when we play Hsueh-feng ourselves. So the question is going to be, how is the Tê-shan part of ourselves, the part that is settled, the part that we admire, the part that we want to be like more of the time, going to get in accord with the Hsueh-feng self-critical part that says, "See, you're still making mistakes." How many times in dokusan do I hear people bringing in some version of that. Even though I *know* this lesson, I'm still making the same mistakes. Over and over and over again.

Now, Yen-t'ou steps up and makes explicit our curative fantasy, the curative fantasy of the last word. If I get *that*, Hsueh-feng will shut up and leave me alone once and for all. In an interview, Joko was once asked, "Do you think some day you'll finally achieve total complete enlightenment, *the anutara samyak sambodhi* in the Heart Sutra?" I can just picture the look on Joko's face when she says, "I hope a thought like that would never even cross my mind." Wu-men's commentary says, "As for the last word, neither Yen-t'ou nor Tê-shan has ever seen it, even in a dream." But Hsueh-feng *has* seen it in his dream, that's the difference. And a lot of us see it in our dreams. It's the fantasy of finally "getting it" in a way that's going to eliminate inner conflict. Ideally, the way we practice is modeled on Tê-shan's reaction to Hsueh-feng; when he's criticized, he says nothing, he just goes back to his room. In that way, he models not taking it personally, just letting it roll off his back. And that's fine, if we can do it. Sometimes we can see that the criticism is empty, and we can just let it go. But other times, even when we see it modeled by a mature teacher, the lesson doesn't sink in. Somehow that non-reactivity by itself doesn't show Hsueh-feng that his criticism was off the mark. Hsueh-feng is reveling in his *gotcha* moment. What it takes to move things along is for Yen-t'ou to step in as a third party and draw out and make explicit what's going on behind the scenes in Hsueh-feng's private curative fantasy.

Yen-t'ou is able to do that because he occupies the position that the psychoanalyst Philip Bromberg calls *standing in the spaces*. We might describe that position as more or less psychicly equidistant between Hsueh-feng and Tê-shan. We could say that he talks the language of both *self-states*. While we're all very familiar with our inner Hsueh-feng and Tê-shan, we often lose track of the role of the inner Yen-t'ou, the part that has to stand in the middle and mediate between the part that we idealize and the part that's critical. It is a fundamental psychological truth that no conflict can ever be resolved by having one side simply eliminate the other. In every conflict, each side represents a motivational interest that ultimately must be acknowledged and given its due. We may long for love and new relationships; equally we may fear rejection and reinjury if we risk trusting anew. We cannot simply *override* our fear. It contains important lessons that only past trauma can teach us, lessons about the reality of danger and impermanence in the world. These lessons must be respected. At the same time, we cannot protect ourselves to the point of living in isolation, for then we will die from the lack of emotional oxygen. Each side must be listened to, each side must have its truths acknowledged.

Dissociation results from our inability, or our unwillingness, to hold conflicting parts of the self in mind at the same time. Although we may experience the conflict between parts of ourselves as painful, conflict is actually the solution, not the problem. We must gradually develop the capacity to forego the relative safety afforded by dissociation and allow ourselves to bear and work through inner conflict. Like a painful or tumultuous family reunion, ultimately everyone must be offered a place at the table.

This case is resolved playfully. Play is one way of standing in the spaces, of having an accepting, ironic distance on the parts of ourselves we normally take to be incompatible. When I first read this case many years ago, it was commonplace to use the Japanese names for the characters. Thus, Hsueh-feng was Seppo, Yen-t'ou was Ganto, and Tê-shan, Tokusan. The names Seppo and Ganto always reminded me of the Marx brothers and made me smile. And if we think about the whole story as a sort of Marx Brothers routine, we'll probably get close to its lesson. Yen-t'ou (Ganto) is playing with Hsueh-feng (Seppo), and Tê-shan (Tokusan) is playing along.

We might have the fantasy that, as the years go by, we are going to become more and more like Tê-shan and nothing's going to affect us. Everything is going to roll off our backs. This is a fantasy of going beyond inner conflict. Is that really what's going to happen in practice? We may imagine that when we're twenty-five (I did), but now thirty or forty years later, most of us are starting to get the idea that that's not what's happening. That's the advantage of finally getting to this age and this stage of practice. You start getting a little more realistic about what's going to happen and what's not going to happen. And one way of summing that up is saying that our inner Hsueh-feng is not going anywhere. The critical part of ourselves, the intrusive part, the part that doesn't conform to our ego ideal is not going away. We have to find some way to come to terms with all parts of ourselves. Now, it's true that Hsueh-feng will go on to become a teacher in his own right and that the critical part of ourselves can mellow into self-reflection. But that can only happen if we learn to accept our own negativity and not fan its flames by adding self-hate on top of self-hate in the name of self-improvement.

This koan is a model of playful engagement with all different aspects of ourselves. What did Yen-t'ou whisper into Tê-shan's ear? Why was Tê-shan different the next day? And what's the last word? If you still want to know, ask yourself, how would Groucho respond?

CHAPTER FIFTEEN

DOING THINGS WITH WORDS

FENG-HSUEH'S SPEECH AND SILENCE

A monk once said to Feng-hsueh, "Speech and silence
tend toward separation from It or concealment of It.
How should we proceed as not to violate It?"
  Feng-hsueh replied with the following verse,
    "I always remember Chiang-nan in the spring,
    the partridges crying
    and the flowers spilling their fragrance."

Although we are repeatedly reminded that Zen is a special transmission outside the sutras, beyond words and concepts, the fact is
language plays a central role in our life and practice. We need to
see reality manifesting in words no less than in rocks and trees.
Even though words are just as empty as rocks and trees, they are
no *more* empty than rocks and trees. The Sandokai reminds us,
"Seeing words you should grasp the great reality." It does not say
see *through* or *beyond* words, or to the reality *behind* words.

A whole class of koans within the traditional system dealt with the
use of language. Unless you are engaged in formal koan study you
are unlikely to encounter them and they are less typically the subject of a teacher's public teishos. Likewise, the traditional Japanese

Rinzai koan curriculum included the use of capping phrases, which involved the student's looking through compilations of quotations of classical literature for one that completed or "capped" the lesson of the koan he had been working on. One of these capping phrase anthologies has been published in English as *The Zen Forest*, but it is unlikely many of us would be capable of making the expected connections given the cultural divides involved.

These koans and the use of capping phrases require us to use language skillfully. Too often students assume that Zen dismisses all language as intrinsically flawed compared to a shout or silence. Yet Chao-chou's use of words was said to be so brilliant that it was as if light played around his lips when he spoke. If, as Zen teacher David Loy suggests, our lives are made of stories, our practice must include the skillful reweaving of our own story. Various kinds of psychotherapy can help us discern how and where we originally learned our personal story and how we have confused it with common sense or just the way life is. We become aware that all stories can be told differently and no story contains the last word (as Hsueh-feng and Yen-t'ou will also remind us).

But we must not imagine that we can be free from language or stories any more than a fish can be free of water. Ultimately, language is our human home. Feng-hsueh, when asked by a monk—who of course was using words in order to ask—how one goes beyond the duality of words and silence, responds spontaneously and unself-consciously with a quote from a famous poem. Today one might say, "April is the cruelest month, breeding / lilacs from the dead ground . . . "

We might contrast this koan with case 39 from the Wu-men kuan, in which a monk begins by saying to Yün-men:

> "Radiant light silently floods the whole universe . . . " But
> Yün-men interrupted him and said, "Aren't you quoting

Zhang Zhuo?" The monk replied, "Yes I am." Yün-men said, "You have misspoken."

Why was this monk wrong to quote an old poem where Feng-hsueh could do so without "misspeaking"? Yün-men evidently could see the monk hadn't made the words his own; they were still someone else's words. But once words come out of my mouth, they are my words, just as much as the air coming out of my nostrils. It doesn't matter that everything I say may have been said before by someone else any more that the air I breathe has been countlessly recycled through other sets of lungs. When I speak, the words are mine.

We are used to thinking of words as creating a picture of the world, a picture that is inevitably arbitrary in terms of what it includes, leaves out, or distorts. But language's function is not exclusively descriptive. The philosopher J. L. Austin reminded us that words can be *performative* as well as representational; that is, they do not solely or merely convey a picture of the world, rather they themselves function as actions within the world. A classic example is when a priest says, "I now pronounce you man and wife." The priest is not *describing* what is in front of him, his words are *performing* a function that alters the reality before him. Austin says these words "do not describe or report . . . anything at all" and therefore "are not true or false." These are not the sort of words that constitute a lens through which we view reality; they themselves are actions that make up our reality. Of course, in many koans, a master's use of a single word can make a life-changing impact, as much as if he literally wielded a stick instead of syllables.

Our relationship to language is also our relationship to our own thought. The quotations I repeat most often are the repetitive thoughts that cycle and recycle around and around in my own mind. I remember when someone asked Joko what her experience of zazen was like after so many years, she replied, "I just sit and think." When Dogen instructed his monks to sit and "think non-thinking," what did he mean? It would be a mistake to translate "think nonthinking" as "don't think." Rather, he is pointing to a way of having a certain relationship or perspective on our thoughts; letting them come and go, the way we let sounds come and go from the outside, as intrinsically empty phenomena that do not need to be either clung to or banished.

Western philosophy after Wittgenstein for a time took what was called "a linguistic turn," and a focus on ordinary language was considered central to untangling what had been thought of as hitherto intractable problems. Maybe some of these were not actually philosophical problems at all but examples of how, in Wittgenstein's phrase, we could be "bewitched by language," tying ourselves into conceptual knots that needed careful unraveling to reveal there was really no problem there after all. The idea was not to reform language, or to imagine there was any way to bypass ordinary speech by using formal logic, but simply to be clear about what we were doing with our words.

J. L. Austin was a one of the original ordinary-language philosophers and his books, in addition to emphasizing the performative function of language mentioned above, often involved tracking the subtle ways language worked in everyday life. This led him on one occasion, while lecturing to a packed house at Columbia University, to remark that in many languages, there are examples of a double negative being used to mean a positive, but that in no language was a double positive ever used to refer to a negative. From the back of the room a voice instantly popped up, "Yeah, yeah."

That voice belonged to Sidney Morgenbesser, a Columbia philosopher known for his Socratic style and dry wit. Like an old Chinese Zen master, he is largely now remembered for just those two words, and nothing he published ever gained the same attention.

This kind of linguistic analysis may not be what most of us think of as philosophy, especially if we think philosophy ought to concern itself with questions about social justice or how we should reshape society to eliminate inequality. But it remains quite relevant when questions about the nature of the self, identity, and personhood bump up against the findings of neurobiology, evolutionary biology, and genetics. What are we to make of the notion of personal responsibility when our genes or our brains appear to have "programmed" us to behave a certain way? How should we respond when someone attempts to explain, deny, or excuse their latest bout of road rage by saying, in effect, "My amygdala made me do it!" Or "That was my low blood-sugar talking"?

The problem, formally known as the *mereological* fallacy, consists in attributing to a part of a person, like the brain, qualities or functions that properly can only be ascribed to the whole person. (*Mereology* is the branch of philosophy concerned with the relation of parts to wholes.) Does it make sense to say that our brains think, believe, understand, interpret, decide, feel, are conscious or unconscious?

This is not a question that calls for *research*. It's a question about language and what it logically makes sense to say. It's a question about what counts as an explanation, what we are doing when we switch from explaining the *reasons* for our actions to describing something "inside" us that is the *cause* of our reasons or our actions. Psychoanalysts are prone to a version of this problem when they ascribe motivation to "the unconscious." It's not that we are not sometimes unconscious or unaware of our own motivations. Rather, instead of seeing that a person sometimes has multiple agendas that may be in conflict with one another and that he may be unable or unwilling to hold all the conflicting states in mind at once, we put a seemingly innocuous "the" in front of the adjective "unconscious" and create a kind of homunculus, a little person inside, with its own motivation and agendas, pulling the levers behind the curtain of awareness, "making" us do all sorts of things we never consciously intended.

Buddhists are, unfortunately but unsurprisingly, just as liable to fall into this trap as anyone else. With us, however, it's not just the brain or our neurochemistry that is behind the curtain, it's "buddha nature" or "true self." But as Joko said, "True self is nothing at all. It's the absence of something else." If there's nothing behind the curtain, maybe we should give all our attention and respect to the curtain itself. Look how it is gently waving in the breeze. Admire its delicate weave, its fine patterns of color and decoration.

Our language, including the language of the Dharma, is part of the flowering of our humanity. It is both an expression of and reflection on who and what we are. It is a garden in which we should play freely. But as the poet Marianne Moore reminded us, imaginary gardens may have real toads in them. What could be more real than our imagination, or the words that make our imagination come to life? If we ourselves are real, how could our words fail to be real as well?

We had better choose them well.

CHAPTER SIXTEEN

INTERGENERATIONAL KARMA

PAI-CHANG AND THE FOX

So much of our practice involves facing what we have thought of as impenetrable barriers, barriers that turn out to exist solely in our imagination. We learn to infuse koans such as Mu with all our frustrations, all our fears of blockage and limitation, so that when they burst open, we find ourselves inhabiting a spaciousness we never imagined possible.

Yet practice is not simply about dissolving boundaries and entering into the limitless sky of the Absolute. Practice must also bring us back down to earth and make us come to terms with the very real limits in our lives. Death, of course, is one such limit that we must all face. History is another. Our personal history, our family history, our cultural history, together make up an inheritance we can, if we wish, refer to with the Buddhist word *karma*.

Karma represents the sum total of cause and effect in our lives; the causes that have made us who we are, the effects we create moment after moment in response to those causes.

The byways of karma in our individual life and within the broader outline of our lineages may be dramatic or subtle. Some Zen lineages, shaken by misconduct, have consciously reconfigured themselves, as Suzuki Roshi's lineage has done at the San Francisco

Zen Center, through a system of co-abbots and term-limits, to avoid concentrating too much power in the person of a single teacher. Other intergenerational dynamics may go unremarked upon and unexamined, unconsciously woven into the fabric of what students take for granted to be the nature of practice. For example, a teacher, who has suffered from the abuse of early caretakers and the unreliability of personal relationships, adopts a stance that valorizes autonomy and asceticism, displaying no need for either people or things.

Is this the result of a deep insightful detachment, or an avoidant adaptation to disappointment? A teacher who suffered the early loss of both parents and entered a monastery at a young age develops a filial devotion to his teacher, the institution of monasticism, and all of the traditions of his sect. Questioning any of these becomes equivalent to disparaging his parents. Loyalty, devotion, and obedience become synonymous with a commitment to the Dharma itself. Is this a life of home-leaving or a life-long project to recreate the home he never had?

The story of Pai-chang and the Fox, which appears as case 2 in the Wu-men kuan, occupies a particularly fitting position following Chao-chou's Mu. Both cases are about freedom, but Mu typically leads to a powerful sense of freedom *from*, while the second case is all about freedom *in the midst of*. Mu frees us from the tyranny of has or has not and reveals the boundlessness beyond dualism. In Mu, nothing is lacking, and the clear sky stretches open in every direction. But this encounter with the Absolute is not only freeing, it can be addictively one-sided. What is needed is a way to bring that freedom out of the sky and down to earth. We need to be able to experience freedom in the midst of our lives, not simply use practice as a way to transcend the limitations of our life.

The old man who comes up to Pai-chang declares that he himself was abbot of the monastery in the time of the legendary buddhas before Shakyamuni, but because he misunderstood the nature of karma, he has been punished by being reborn as a fox over five hundred lifetimes. The key question, which he now poses to Pai-chang (and to us) in turn, is "Is the enlightened man free from cause and effect?" Here we have the crux of the matter: from what does realization free us? What would it mean to be free from karma, from the law of cause and effect?

Once, when our sesshin happened to fall on Passover, I announced I would be giving a teisho on case 2½ of the Gateless Gate, "Magid and the Old Jew." In this version of the story, an old man with a long white beard, dressed in a black coat and fur hat, who has been sitting at the back of the hall, as far away as possible from the women, comes up after the teisho and says:

> Many years ago, I was a Ju-Bu (Jewish-born Buddhist) like you, and was abbot of this monastery. I had put all my Jewish past behind me, so when someone asked me whether the enlightened man transcended cause and effect, I replied yes, he did. As a result I have been reborn for five hundred lifetimes as a Hasid. Now tell me: Does the enlightened man transcend his past?

Karma, or cause and effect, means our history, both in the personal sense of my own deeds and their consequences and also the whole familial, cultural, and historical chains of events that have led me to being who I am today. We all have ambivalent feelings about our pasts, and as American Buddhists, almost all of us have left, to one degree or another, the tradition in which we grew up in order to practice Zen. Americans, ironically, seem to have a long history of wanting to start over, to wipe the slate clean and begin afresh, a legacy that stretches from Ellis Island to such archetypal reinventors of themselves as Jay Gatsby and Don Draper. It is as if we have a tradition of periodically dissociating ourselves from our own history.

My own name, Magid, is derived from the Hebrew word for teacher, and if you look into Martin Buber's *Tales of the Hasidim*, you will find many Maggids there, sometimes engaged in rather Zen-like mondos. My father's family left Russia on a boat that landed in Montreal, and the French influence there softened the *g* so that my name is now pronounced in an unusual and non-Hebrew fashion. But in some ways, as a Zen teacher, I am continuing in the old family business.

In other ways, as a Buddhist American, I am living a life that would be unrecognizable (and no doubt unacceptable) to my for-bears. What is my relationship to my Jewish past? Has that slate been wiped clean? The koan suggests if we imagine we can do so, we will be in for a shock, as we will be made to relive our past one way or another. Certainly the Jews of my parents and grandparents generation in Europe learned that no matter how assimilated they felt themselves to be to European culture, their Jewishness would prove inescapable when Hitler came to power.

Wu-men's comment on this koan suggests that the old man lived happily in his five hundred lives as a fox, and this points us to the idea that we can be free in the midst of our karma, rather than needing to transcend it. Both in the realm of physics and the realm of psychology, nothing is either created or destroyed; the building blocks of matter and energy that make up the universe are endlessly reshuffled. As I have tried to show over and over in the previous chapters, nothing is ever truly expelled from our mind, and this koan likewise shows us that nothing is ever truly expelled from our history either.

As we proceed to create a hybridization of American psychologi-cally minded culture and Asian Buddhist practice, we will inevitably create incongruities, like the matzoh in the *oryoki* bowls at our

Passover sesshin. Perhaps there is a place for the re-creation of a traditional Japanese monastery on American soil, but for the vast majority of contemporary American lay practitioners, the whole point of bringing Zen to the West is to produce mongrels, new breeds that will blend features of our past and our present in ways that will be largely uncontrollable and unpredictable. We cannot transcend our past, but neither can we keep some idealized version of it frozen in the amber of "authenticity" or "tradition."

Asian Buddhism is preoccupied with lineage and continuity in a way that serves as both contrast and corrective to a Western, and especially, American desire to always make it new. In our zendo, we chant a service in both English and the traditional Sino-Japanese. Although my teacher taught in Southern California, we do not pretend that Zen was invented there. We shall not forget where we came from or how we got here.

If we did, who knows how we might be reborn.

CHAPTER SEVENTEEN

USELESSNESS

THE KOAN OF JUST SITTING

Eihei Dogen said, "Zazen is not a meditation technique. It is simply the Dharma gate of joyful ease; it is practicing the realization of the boundless Dharma way. Here, the open mystery manifests, and there are no more traps and snares for you to get caught in."

Over and over, the great thirteenth-century Zen master Eihei Dogen emphasized that practice and realization are from the beginning inseparable. Not that the practice of zazen is an uniquely efficacious tool for achieving realization, but that zazen itself, from the moment of our first beginner's instruction, is the complete manifestation of the Awakened Way. This assertion, which formed the very heart of his own realization and teaching, is deeply counterintuitive when we first hear it and probably remains so for a long time thereafter. Zazen itself, the practice of just sitting, genuinely deserves to be called a koan, an expression of opposites we are challenged to dissolve.

What do we mean by "just sitting"? "Sitting" means sitting, walking, working, eating, speaking, and being silent. "Just" means that there is nothing in the world that is not sitting.

Thus when we speak of just sitting, we are not limiting ourselves to describing a particular posture or practice. We are describing a way of being in the world in which everything we encounter is fully and completely itself. Nothing is merely a means to an end, nothing is merely a step on the path to somewhere else. Every moment, everything, is absolutely foundational in its own right. Zazen, defined in the narrow sense as seated meditation, is but one of an infinite number of possible paradigms for this state, yet at the same time, for Dogen at least, it is the unique expression of the coming together of the human nature and buddha nature. Yet because our every action is also zazen, in Dogen's vision of the monastic life, we sacramentalize and ritualize every aspect of daily life, from sitting in the zendo to working in the kitchen to washing ourselves in the toilet.

If we think of one of the central functions of the koan as being to illuminate and then deconstruct our habitual tendency to dualistic thinking in all the ways that we dichotomize our life, then "just sitting" becomes a way of expressing the resolution of the koan of everyday life at its most fundamental level. This is what Dogen called *genjokoan*, actualization in everyday life. It is in the explication of genjokoan that Dogen utters his most famous summary of life and practice:

> To study the buddha way is to study the self. To study the self is to forget the self. To forget the self is to be actualized by myriad things. When actualized by myriad things, your body and mind as well as the bodies and minds of others drop away. No trace of realization remains, and this no-trace continues endlessly. When you first seek Dharma, you imagine you are far away from its environs. At the moment when Dharma is correctly transmitted, you are immediately your original self.

Condensed in these words is the entirely of our life and practice. We begin, as in so many koans, with a dichotomy we have created in our own mind between the "Buddha Way" and our "self," as if they were separate entities, worlds apart, and practice was somehow a matter of making the twain meet. So Dogen begins by asserting that to study the one is to study the other. Rather than being opposed or incompatible, they are, in fact, inextricable. Yet, because we do not know what either the Buddha Way or the self truly is, our understanding of each must undergo a transformation.

That transformation begins in the next line; to study the self is to forget the self. A strange sort of study that leads us to forget the subject of our study.

I am reminded of Lawrence Weschler's biography of the artist Robert Irwin, which was titled *Seeing Is Forgetting the Name of the Thing One Sees*. This kind of study, this kind of seeing, involves a loss of boundaries, a letting go of our stance as a separate, objective observer, and instead places us in the midst of the very landscape we say we are studying. Or, we might say, that when we attempt to "study" our "self," we find, as Shakyamuni did before us, that there is nothing we can pin down and call our "self" that is not constantly changing, constantly being constituted and reconstituted by ever-shifting interactions with the whole world.

Dogen calls this interpenetration of self and world "being actualized by myriad things." "Actualized" means being called into being, or being made what we most truly are. When we cannot find any boundary between ourselves and the myriad things, our mind, our body, the bodies and mind of others, all "drop away"—any distinction, any separate "having" becomes a fiction we no longer maintain. Where there is no separate body or mind, there also can be no separate realization. "Realization" isn't some change taking place privately inside my personal consciousness; it is instead the experience of from-the-beginning embeddedness in all of life, an embeddedness with no beginning and no end, which "continues endlessly."

The last sentence returns us to where we started, "When you first seek the Dharma, you imagine you are far away from its environs." This recapitulates our initial misconception of dichotomizing Buddha Way and self. "But when the Dharma is correctly transmitted, you are immediately your original self." The gap is closed.

The Dharma is neither far away nor is it something that we had been lacking and now have found. Our original self, the self-in-the-world that we have always been, is unceasingly revealing the Buddha Way in every moment. Nothing was hidden; what we have found has been in plain sight all along.

Dogen's vision of the unity of practice and realization is often considered the height of esoterica; a mystical view that we ordinary types can barely fathom. Indeed the record of his talks that have come down to us as the Shobogenzo, the "Treasury of the True Dharma Eye," contains language that is deeply elusive, paradoxical, and ungraspable by any ordinary logic. What relevance can this perspective have for our day-to-day psychological issues?

Let's go back to the beginning where Dogen introduces the practice of zazen. He emphasizes that it is not a technique of meditation, and this seemingly paradoxical assertion will open many doors for us if we will follow its implications to the end. It is one of the most ingrained and unconsciously pernicious of our psychological habits to treat almost everything we do as a means to an end. Like a small child in the back seat of a car on a long drive, our habitual lament is "Are we there yet?"

If we truly engage Kodo Sawaki's assertion that "Zazen is useless," we discover that doing this useless thing is profoundly different from everything else we do in our lives. It may, in fact, be the only useless thing we ever do. Our whole lives are organized around one purpose or another. Everything we do has a purpose, whether it's to earn money, have a good time, or do good for others. Everything we do can thus be judged on some scale of accomplishment. *How am I doing?* There is always answer, sometimes out to three decimal points. We are so used to everything having a purpose, we may even find ourselves asking the question, "What is the purpose of life itself?" We'll never find the answer to that one because the question itself makes no sense. We have hopelessly conflated "purpose" with meaning and value.

This is why it can be so hard to answer when our friends or relatives ask us why we practice Zen. The question presumes that Zen is a technique with a purpose, a practice with something as its goal. "Does it make you calm or happy?" Like any koan, it doesn't work to answer either yes or no. If like Bodhidharma we reply, "I don't know," we will probably leave our questioner as confused as the emperor.

If zazen is truly useless, the first moment we do it, just as Dogen says, we have entered into a totally different realm. We are instantaneously off the grid, so to speak, of means and ends, of progress and goals. We are in a whole new world where what we are doing is not, cannot, be justified by something outside of itself, by what it's going to get us, or where it's going to take us. We just sit. We just are. Perhaps as we sit we will realize that everything in the world, from myself to the morning star, is equally useless and has no justification, no reason or meaning outside of itself.

In our scientifically minded age, the apotheosis of the idea that everything must be a means to an end is evolutionary biology. Every aspect of our existence as human beings, we are assured, is the way it is because somewhere along the line it conveyed a selective evolutionary advantage. Our hands, our minds, our taste for sweets all evolved in their current form because long ago on some hypothetical African savannah, some ancestor of ours was able to reproduce more successfully, more prolifically, than his fellows because of a mutation granting this new trait.

Do we believe that even the capacity to meditate is such a trait? We can make up a just-so story that meditation is a byproduct of the capacity to sit still and concentrate, and the first meditators were hunters sitting absolutely still and silent while they stalked their game. The most patient, concentrated hunter might indeed have an advantage over the competition. But how do we understand it when that capacity "evolves" to the point where those who are most drawn to silence and stillness and concentration forget about hunting and decide to become celibate monastics?

Can we concoct a just-so story that gives evolutionary advantage to celibacy? It certainly sounds like a contradiction in terms. Biologists have long struggled with the question as to whether the unit of evolution can be something other than the individual. Does having a monk—or homosexual—in the family somehow give the family, and thereby those carrying a large portion of the monk's genes, some advantage over other families not so blessed? Does a society in which a significant percentage of the population chooses to become celibate contemplatives have some evolutionary advantage over another competing society where most men become warriors? I'm sure there's an evolutionary biologist out there somewhere who can concoct an explanation, but I prefer to think that at a certain point some traits simply are cut loose from their evolutionary moorings and drift free into uselessness. Maybe that means they won't be around in another ten thousand or hundred thousand years.

Or maybe human beings will only be around at all if enough of us become Buddhists and save the planet. A real but I suspect too indirect advantage for Darwinians to invoke.

I have gone down this little evolutionary byway to suggest how hard it is for us to step outside means-to-an-end thinking. (No doubt because means-to-an-end thinking in the right contexts conveys some evolutionary advantage!) Yet Dogen has shown us the way out of this cul-de-sac in one fell swoop. The moment we sit down to do zazen, we are useless, what we are doing has no point outside of itself, outside of the moment itself. We just are, we just sit, and in the very act of sitting, we actualize the completeness of the act itself and we actualize our own full completeness as a useless human being, another name for which is Buddha.

CHAPTER EIGHTEEN

WHOLENESS VS. WHOLESOMENESS

THE PRECEPTS

Broadly speaking, religious practice traditionally is concerned with *goodness*, about perfecting and purifying our character, while psychological practice focuses instead on *wholeness*, the capacity to own or experience every aspect of our self-experience, without repression, dissociation, or denial. What I call *wholesomeness* centers on changing and perfecting (however we define that word) the content of our mind and of our behavior, while *wholeness* is about total self-acceptance, regardless of the content.

Freud's project centered on the long difficult process of acknowledgment of all the aspects of our fantasies, dreams, and motivations that we would ordinarily deny or disown. By placing the myth of Oedipus at the metaphorical heart of his psychoanalytic theory, Freud asserted that the most forbidden of sexual wishes and the most heinous of murderous impulses were the undeniable and universal truth about what it was to be human.

The Four Noble Truths likewise asserted that there was something at the heart of what it meant to be human—something that has variously been translated as desire, clinging, or ignorance— that gave rise to a universal experience of suffering. However, the

Eightfold Path promised a way out of suffering by regulating life in accord with the twin realities of interconnection and impermanence.

In the form of the Vinaya, the elaborate rules set down to define and structure a monastic way of life, the precepts serve to deliberately create a way of life distinct from that of ordinary people. The Buddha said that his monks should live like an island unto themselves in the midst of the world. It is meant to be a life manifesting the reality of impermanence, a life of no fixed abode and no possessions. It is meant to be a life free from attachment and desire, a life without familial or sexual relations.

After formal meals during meditation retreats, we chant, "May we exist like a lotus, at home in muddy water." One way of understanding this is that we should strive to be the one pure thing in an impure world, to rise above the muddy water of greed, anger, and ignorance and manifest the pure lotus-like life of the Dharma. The life of a monk can serve as an inspiration to us all, showing how it is possible to lead life without clinging to all those things we ordinarily are sure we can't live without. Yet the monastic life outlined by the *Vinaya* has two inherent dilemmas associated with it.

The first is that it is dependent on the wider community of non-monks for support by alms. When Buddhism moved to China and the life of the wandering bhikkhu was replaced by the life within the stable confines of a monastery—a change attributed to Pai-chang—the monastic ideal was reformulated to be grounded in self-sufficiency rather than being dependent on alms. "A day of no work is a day of no eating" became the new maxim. This change also served to eliminate one difference between the life of monks as subsistence farmers and the life of the peasantry surrounding them. A second dilemma inherent in the picture of monasticism as a self-contained form of the ideal life is that it is dependent on outsiders—if not for alms, then for the next generation of monks, since monks by definition do not reproduce.

Like Tolstoy's *The Kreutzer Sonata*, the Vinaya presents an ideal life that if adopted by everyone who lead literally to the end of life. It is in some ways the inverse of Kant's categorical imperative to act in such a way that your action could serve as the basis of a universal law. The Vinaya describes an ethical absolute that can function only because everyone does *not* adopt it. But it's a big world, and it is not unfair to say that monks will always only be a part, not the whole, of it and that there is nothing unreasonable about adopting a code to define and separate the life of monastics from that of lay people. The irony is that the foundation of the Buddhist view of life is *nonseparation.*

By contrast, in our Ordinary Mind form of lay Buddhist practice, the precepts function to remind of our embeddedness in the world as it is, not to help us stand apart from it. We are engaged in a fundamental transformation of one of the core concepts of practice from the time of the Buddha; a reevaluation of the centrality of home-leaving. Contemporary lay practice is premised on the belief that the Dharma may be fully practiced, realized, and transmitted entirely within the context of lay life.

One consequence of this shift in perspective is that the role of the teacher is increasingly separate from the functions of a priest and that ordination is no longer a prerequisite part of the training of Zen teachers in many lineages. Lay practice centers may have as their leaders fully transmitted lay teachers and may or may not maintain affiliation with priest-led temples. Services at lay practices centers may be performed entirely by the lay members themselves, without any service positions reserved exclusively for priests. Even ceremonies like jukai, the giving of the precepts, are increasingly recognized as embodying a commitment to a life of practice that may be defined and maintained entirely within a circle of lay practitioners without the need for priestly validation.

What then is the role of priests and monastics in contemporary American Zen Buddhism? There are many answers to this question and many of those answers are in a state of flux, evolution, and even controversy. Some lineages, like the Soto lineage of Suzuki Roshi, have been very reluctant to acknowledge the autonomy of lay practice and transmission, while others, like the Sanbo Kyodan lineage of Aitken Roshi's teacher, Yamada Koun, were founded precisely to be lay lineages.

The meaning of being a priest, a monastic, and a teacher is being worked out differently in different lineages. It is clear however that only a very small percentage of practitioners are, or could, follow a path of lifelong monasticism. Many students, particularly when they start out, are able to devote anywhere from a few months to a few years to a period of residential training before returning to their education, job, and family back "in the world." One may live residentially for a time without becoming a monk, just as one may learn the traditional forms and perform various services within the sangha or the larger community without becoming a priest. Speaking for myself, being a priest means that is your primary occupation. One would not hold an outside job or have another means of livelihood. A priest thus requires a practice community that is financially capable of providing full-time support for the priest and his or her family.

Being a priest, in this way of looking at things, is also distinct from being a monk, whose life would be further organized around a different set of vows, which typically would include poverty and chastity, and whose practice is not oriented outward to the needs of the surrounding community, but directed inward toward her own spiritual quest and to the rigors of training within the context of a residential center.

In all of this I find myself in agreement with one of my former teachers, Bernie Glassman, who has said:

> My feeling had always been that you were a priest if you
> had a temple to run and take care of. Not a zendo. If what

you were doing was concentrating on meditation and zendo aspects, you don't have to be a priest. . . . I had seen so many people ordaining that had no connection with running a temple. They were doing their work and then they would become Zen teachers, but it didn't make any sense to me why you need all those priests besides there being this historical precedence within the Japanese Soto sect that says in order to be a teacher you have to be a priest. . . . Now, I do feel you need priests, but the priests should be people who have temples, and running a temple in the Soto sect means holding three services a day; very few priests that I know do that. Most of the people that I know that are priests have nothing to do with temple life. They have other jobs. . . . I felt that as priests that should be their vocation: they should be working at a temple. They might or might not be a teacher. You can be a great priest but a lousy teacher. I see them as two separate tracks and I actually make the studies and the paths that way.

A nonordained lay teacher like myself is not financially sup-ported by the community except in a nominal sense; my main live-lihood comes from my work as a psychoanalyst. If the community can afford it, a full-time priest living at the center or temple can provide a wonderful model for the life of practice and anchor the practice of the entire sangha by the example of her own daily prac-tice and commitment. If only for practical reasons, this is a model that fewer and fewer practice centers can afford to adopt. We do not have in America, as in Japan, the tradition of Zen temples being supported by the larger community, typically through their conducting of funeral services or other community functions, or of broader community patronage. A few of the larger Zen centers may continue to function in this way, but more and more alternatives are springing up as people in all walks of life become interested in integrating meditation into their daily lives.

In the context of our lay practice, the precepts are not so much vows of conduct or rules of behavior as a way of *bearing witness* to life as it is. We bear witness to the evils enumerated in the precepts the way we bear witness to the reality of old age and death. Witnessing does not preclude or replace the need to do what we can to ameliorate suffering. We do all we can to heal the sick and ease the pain of dying. But we do not imagine it our task to eliminate the fact of sickness, old age, or death from the world, nor do we condemn life itself for including these elements. We do not hate life for including suffering nor do we bitterly resign ourselves to its reality.

We *bear witness* to the reality of killing all around us, and acknowledge that our life is inevitably grounded in the killing of other life, plant and animal. We *bear witness* to the reality of theft manifest as inequality in the world, and acknowledge that what we possess and enjoy and use to make our own life secure is gained at the expense of those less fortunate than ourselves. We *bear witness* to the reality of sexuality, which, fueled by unconscious fantasy and desire, will always contain transgressive elements that resist domestication and erupt in ways that disrupt our ideals of intimacy and mutuality. We *bear witness* to how our basic human need for love divides the world into those who are special to us and those to whom we long to be special. We *bear witness* to all the ways our own personal history of suffering has led us to distrust one another and to distrust life itself, causing us to separate ourselves and withhold our wholehearted participation in life out of fear of being disappointed and hurt once again.

Fundamentally, we bear witness to the reality of our own needs, desires, vulnerabilities, and the reality of our being creatures who exist simultaneously in the realms of separation and embeddedness. A changing, interconnected world whiplashes us between our experience of ourselves as separate individuals and as participants in a seamless whole. We must come to terms with both sides of our nature. Practice will not lead us into a state of harmony by eliminating some aspect of who we are.

We are not practicing to denature ourselves—to "breed vegetarian tigers," as it were. Anyone who has attended a Rinzai Zen sesshin knows that Buddhist practice can *channel* aggression and a love for toughness and endurance but does not eliminate it. Nor should it, especially when you are trying to shape the character of testosterone-driven adolescents and young men. How to appropriately channel their sexuality, rather than try to either repress it altogether or dissociate it into split-off night-time behavior (like after work drinking) that doesn't "count" to their day-time practice persona—this is a koan that remains to be solved.

The precepts are traditionally taken up as the culmination of koan practice. Having spent years in a form of life meant to embody the fulfillment of the precepts, one must finally engage the precepts from the perspective from which they *can't* be broken. This is the perspective from which the task of saving all beings is already fulfilled, for all beings intrinsically are buddhas, and any dichotomy between being deluded and saved is empty. In Dogen's terms, just as zazen is not a means to an end, not a technique for becoming enlightened, the precepts are not rules for living an ethical life so much as a expression of the realized life, the way we function from the point of view of actualized nonseparation. This also seems to have been the attitude of Hui-neng (or whoever authored the Platform Sutra), who (in the words of Buddhist scholar Paul Groner) called "into question the sequentialist understanding of precepts, meditation and wisdom." That text, with its depiction of Hui-neng's full realization while still a layman, and his offering of a simplified version of the precepts to laymen and monks alike, grounded the precepts in the underlying truth of nonduality, which when realized, spontaneously gives rise to right action.

From this perspective, we say there is just life as it is, a seamless whole. If we think of this life as infinity, nothing can be added or subtracted from it. Infinity plus one is infinity. Infinity minus one is infinity. Infinity divided in two is still infinity. From this vantage point, there is no killing, no stealing, no harming of any kind. No one to kill or be killed; nothing to steal, gain, or lose.

The Great Vows for All—the four bodhisattva vows—also serve as koans to illuminate this point. Is saving all beings an endless task stretching from lifetime to lifetime, or has it already been accomplished this very instant? Do our inexhaustible delusions have any real substance at all? If not, how are they any different from the myriad other momentary dharmas that arise and fall in each and every moment? What mastery of these dharmas can there be other than allowing them to come and go? All beings, without exception, partake of the emptiness and interconnectedness we call buddha nature. What else can we possibly embody other than the Buddha Way?

It would be a terrible mistake, however, to take this interpretation of the precepts and Great Vows as the equivalent of one great vow of complacency. We are not saying that because we already embody the Buddha Way there is no need to practice. As Suzuki Roshi told his students, "Each one of you is perfect the way you are and you can use a little improvement." The deep acceptance of life as it is—including our mind as it is—is a starting point, not an end point. We can all use the ongoing structure—and sometimes the strictures—of vow and discipline to unmask the subtle ways that our cravings and attachments implicitly reject the moment in favor of some imagined version of how life is supposed to be, how we are supposed to be able to feel.

Throughout this book, I have emphasized the transformative

power of staying with all those aspects of the self we normally split off, both consciously and unconsciously. My sense of the precepts likewise arises out of the sense that they function at the deepest level to remind us of all sides of our true nature, what is most human and vulnerable and simultaneously what is most perfect and complete. Although we all will fall short of the ideal of non-self-centeredness they represent, I do not believe we can radically transform ourselves by interpreting them as stringent reminders to curb our appetites. Those who engage in greed, egotistical self-aggrandizement, or sexual misconduct have not forgotten the the prohibitions against these behaviors. Rather, the needs and longings that give rise to these transgressions have been so disowned, so split off, that they can only erupt in a clandestine or highly rationalized fashion, with the individuals often maintaining to the end their own righteousness.

As we develop new ways to enter the stream of the Dharma in the midst of everyday life, the precepts are undergoing a shift away from being explicit rules of conduct and toward being a broader perspective on life as it is. We chant these vows as a way of simultaneously acknowledging both an ideal we aspire to and a reality that is already present even if we fail to recognize it.

CHAPTER NINETEEN

SURRENDER & SUBMISSION

NO HEAT OR COLD

A monk asked Tung-shan (Jap. Tozan), "When cold and heat come, how does one avoid them?"

Tung-shan said, "Why not go to where there is no cold or heat?"

The monk said, "How is it when there is no cold or heat?"

Tung-shan said, "When it's cold, it kills you with cold; when it's hot, it kills you with heat."

When I first began sitting with a sangha, all of whom were Americans, led by a Japanese teacher, we had a habit of answering *"Hai!"* whenever we were told to do something. *"Hai,"* which is Japanese for "yes," was just about the only Japanese word we knew—except for *"kensho"* of course—and the joke was that we would never be told what the word for "no" was because we would never need it.

The habit of reflexively saying "yes" is actually a very good practice. It can help make us aware of how often we unconsciously let ourselves back away from what is being asked of us through anxiety, fear, or more subtle forms of avoidance. Joko always taught us to pay attention to those subtle moments of hesitation, those moments when we try to say "no" instead of "yes" to life in an attempt to manage our insecurity.

The koan that opens this chapter is likewise about saying "yes" to everything, especially to those things that we come to practice seeking to avoid. The monk wants to know how to avoid cold and heat and instead is told let the cold kill him, let the heat kill him. We're not just talking literally about cold and heat here, of course. We are talking about cold and heat as examples of what we are afraid we can't handle and of all the likes and dislikes that practice is meant to confront. It's important to notice that the monk asks about cold and heat as a pair; at a metaphorical level he's asking about all the dualisms we confront, from life and death to liking and disliking. And the monk's question posits the existence of a place *beyond* those dualisms, a particular curative fantasy that Tung-shan makes explicit, leading the monk on, when he asks, "Why not go to where there is no cold or heat?"

Is there such a place? Can we reach a different state of consciousness in our sitting where we transcend all duality, where pain and pleasure dissolve as opposites? In one sense, we can. In moments of total concentration or absorption, we can leave behind all our everyday likes and dislikes. And what happens then? We immediately compare this state with our ordinary state of mind and decide, "I like this one much better." And we're right back where we started in the realm of likes and dislikes. No, this koan is not about going into a state of oneness beyond the dualities of cold and heat and somehow staying there full time, though perhaps that is the fantasy behind the monk's question. Exposing that sort of fantasy is the real work we have to do in ourselves with a koan like this, exposing the curative fantasy of transcendence in whatever form in takes in our own lives. How we all secretly wish to go *beyond* . . .

We could say this koan exemplifies the collision of that transcendental fantasy with surrender to reality. "Surrender" is another word for completely saying "yes" to every moment, a "yes" so total we lose ourselves in it. In Tung-shan's way of speaking, we let it "kill" us as a separate self who stands in any way apart from the experience itself, liking or disliking it.

Surrender is a total letting go, and as such it lies at the heart of many spiritual practices and traditions. Yet in light of our current psychological thinking, we can also see that it sometimes stands in an uneasy relation to submission and obedience. Monks in a Catholic monastery take a formal vow of obedience to the rule and to the abbot, turning over their will to God's representative. Not my will but Thy will be done is a fundamental principle for overcoming the tyranny of ego. But what about when the abbot himself acts like a tyrant? Thomas Merton spent years in conflict with his abbot, who refused his requests for more time in solitude, and with the Church hierarchy, who for years refused permission for him to publish anything relating to issues of social justice, race, or the Vietnam War.

Can obedience to any authority, no matter how arbitrary, be made into a useful practice for overcoming my own egotism? Is there any point at all where I have to be able to say "no"? It is perhaps not irrelevant to that question that the teacher who taught his students to always say *"Hai!"* was later embroiled in charges of sexual misconduct.

Untangling the relationship between surrender and submission is no easy task. Psychoanalyst Emanuel Ghent has suggested that the longing for liberation inherent in genuine surrender lies behind the maladaptive compromises involved in submission and masochism. He went so far as to call masochism a "perversion" of surrender, a way in which our longing for genuine release at the deepest level is hijacked by submission to another person's will. How can we recognize genuine surrender? Here are some of the characteristics that Ghent used to distinguish it from submission:

1. It does not necessarily require another person's presence, except possibly as a guide. One may surrender "in the presence of another," not "to another" as in the case of submission.

2. Surrender is not a voluntary activity. One cannot choose to surrender, though one can choose to submit. One can provide facilitative conditions for surrender but cannot make it happen.

3. It may be accompanied by a feeling of dread and death, and/or clarity, relief, even ecstasy.

4. It is an experience of being "in the moment," totally in the present, where past and future, the two tenses that require "mind" in the sense of secondary processes, have receded from consciousness.

5. Its ultimate direction is the discovery of one's identity, one's sense of self, one's sense of wholeness, even one's sense of unity with other living beings. This is quite unlike submission in which the reverse happens: one feels one's self as a puppet in the power of another; one's sense of identity atrophies.

6. In surrender there is an absence of domination and control; the reverse is true in the case of submission. It is easily confused with submission and often confounded with it for exploitative purposes. Certainly in life they are often found together. Considering the central thesis of this paper, that submission be viewed as a defensive mutant of surrender, this juxtaposition should not be surprising. (Nonetheless they are intrinsically very different.)

8. The distinction I am making between surrender and submission helps clarify another pair that are often confused. Resignation accompanies submission; it is heavy and lugubrious. Acceptance can only happen with surrender. It transcends the conditions that evoked it. It is joyous in spirit and, like surrender, it happens; it cannot be made to happen.

I have written elsewhere about how resignation feels like a dead end. Acceptance, on the other hand, feels like a starting point. Yet how often do we fail to distinguish them and find ourselves trying to "accept" something that is extinguishing our hope or vitality? Killing the "ego"—if it's to lead to genuine surrender in Ghent's sense—cannot be equivalent to crushing our spirit.

We yearn to "let go," but that yearning can be exploited by those who have unacknowledged desires to be dominant and in control. The repeated episodes of sexual misconduct by spiritual teachers can be understood as just such a perversion or exploitation of the student's longing for surrender. As Ghent says:

> Erotic fantasies in relation to the analyst (usually, but by no means only, in the case of a female patient with male analyst) or the wish to make love with the analyst so very often turns out to have as its root the intense longing to surrender in the sense of giving over, yielding the defensive superstructure, being known, found, penetrated, recognized.

Psychoanalytic studies of masochism can also provide us with some important insights into how people allow themselves to be drawn into what, to outside observers, look like inexplicable acts of sometimes literally painful submission. What they tell us, first of all, is that masochism needs to be understood, not as a case of a person's seeking pain for its own sake, but as the byproduct of an individual believing that he must pay an increasingly painful cost for the love, attention, or recognition he is desperately seeking.

Another term for masochism is "pathological accommodation," which refers to a progressive sacrifice of one's own vital needs in the service of maintaining a relationship without which, one imagines, one cannot survive. Like the frog, who it is said can be boiled alive if placed in water that is very slowly heated to the boiling point, a person in a masochistically submissive relationship may make one compromise, one sacrifice after another, that cumulatively lead to the equivalent of emotional death. Like the female protagonist in the erotic masterpiece *The Story of O*, a person may engage in a series of painful sacrifices in the hope of holding the attention of an idealized object, wanting to become special through the degree or totality of her commitment or submission. This is the defining difference between submission and surrender: submission is tied to eliciting a response in another person, whether simple approval, love, or just an absence of criticism or abuse. True surrender, on the other hand, has no goal. Like Tung-shan says, it "kills" completely any expectation or gaining idea.

It may seem like an metaphorical stretch to go from a fable of erotic masochism like "O" to the life of a Zen monk, yet all too often the path of pathological accommodation can be the same, with a longing for spiritual attainment or specialness in the eyes of an idealized master substituting for erotic longing. The recurrence of sexual misconduct in spiritual communities is one sign of how blurred the lines between personal, spiritual, emotional, and physical surrender can become. But one does not have to go to the point of sexual abuse to be engaged in unhealthy forms of submission.

As a psychoanalyst, I have seen a number of cases of Buddhist students who have had to leave residential communities because of chronic depression. Almost inevitably, these students have blamed themselves for their failure and have a great deal of trouble sorting out what has happened to bring them to their impasse. Their depression often seems based in what Ghent says about resignation: it has arisen from years of submission that have failed to give rise to genuine surrender and acceptance. Their teachers, sadly, all too often have no understanding of the role they themselves have played in creating this condition and their failure to acknowledge their own enacting of the domination side in a unhealthy dominant-submissive dyad leaves the student made to feel the fault lies in entirely in herself and her own personal psychopathology.

Students in such circumstances are stuck between a rock and a hard place. Their relationship with their teacher, which, at this point can be totally identified with their life of practice, is too precious to give up. All their ideals, devotion, and meaning in life have become centered on holding on at all costs. Yet doing so is progressively draining, as some vital emotional need is repeatedly denied or repudiated in the process. Any protest or expression of longing may be squashed by the teacher as further evidence of the student's emotional instability or unhealthy attachment. Sometimes it is the very students who for years were considered the "best" that turn out to be suffering the most, as years of compliance eventually begin to take their toll.

These impasses are familiar to psychoanalysts, who (sometimes belatedly) have learned that they must look for the unspoken, unacknowledged ways in which a seemingly "good" analysis has led the patient down an unintended byway of submission and compliance. By trying to be "good" patients, who will hold the analyst's attention, win his love or ward off his abandonment, they have learned (sometimes consciously, sometimes unconsciously), to repress "unacceptable" parts of themselves in the analyst's presence. Some things, particularly about how the analyst has been inattentive, critical, or just plain wrong, become unsayable. The emperor's new clothes are always admired. The analysis then becomes a parody of itself, going through the motions, but having no real traction at the level of the unspoken agendas that are really driving it. This dynamic, I believe, has been reenacted over and over again in many Zen teaching centers. Compliance masquerades as non-selfcenteredness, submission as devotion, masochism as aspiration.

The key to breaking out of this pattern is for the analyst or teacher to acknowledge his or her own role in creating it. Unless we are prepared to admit that our own good intentions may mask a deeper unconscious need to always be seen as good, as always right, as always clear, we will never be able to acknowledge the ways that we have inadvertently hurt the very people we are trying to help. *The teacher's own goodness is unconsciously preserved by having the patient or student always be in the wrong. They* are one who is being defensive, deluded, or attached. I remember Joko's sly comment on a fellow teacher. "There's nothing wrong with so-and-so. He just thinks he's enlightened."

The only way out of this impasse is to re-own all those parts of ourselves that we have projected onto the other. We have to remember the wisdom of the old Walt Kelly cartoon character Pogo, who (in a strip published at the height of the Vietnam war) proclaimed, "We have met the enemy, and he is us."

CHAPTER TWENTY

SELF-SACRIFICE VS. COMPASSION

TOREI ENJI'S "BODHISATTVA'S VOW"

When I, a student of the Way,
Look at the real form of the universe,
All is the never-failing manifestation
Of the mysterious truth of the Awakened Life.
In any event, in any moment, and in any place,
None can be other than
The marvelous revelation of its glorious light.
This realization made our ancestors and teachers
Extend tender care, with respectful hearts,
Even to such beings as birds and beasts.
This realization teaches us
That our daily food, drink, clothes,
And protections of life are the warm flesh and blood,
The merciful incarnation of the Awakened One.
Who can be ungrateful or not respectful,
Even to senseless things, not to speak of human beings.
Even though he may be a fool,
Be warm and compassionate toward him.
If by any chance he should turn against us,
Become a sworn enemy and abuse and persecute us,

We should sincerely bow down with humble language,
In the reverent understanding
That he is the merciful manifestation
Of the Awakened One,
Who uses devices to emancipate us
From blind tendencies, produced and accumulated upon
ourselves,
By our own egoistic delusion and attachment,
Through countless cycles of space and time.
Then on each moment's flash of our thought,
There will grow a lotus flower,
And on each lotus flower will be revealed Perfection,
Unceasingly manifest as our life, just as it is,
Right here and right now.
May we extend this mind to all beings,
So that we and the world together
May attain maturity in the wisdom of the Awakened Life.

The corollary to an unhealthy *submission* to others is an unhealthy *devotion* to others at the expense of one's own legitimate emotional and physical needs—a parody of compassion that I have called *vowing to save all being minus one*. As I have discussed earlier, we may enlist our practice and our attempts at being compassionate in the service of a curative fantasy of eliminating our own neediness and vulnerability. Unable to face need in ourselves, we project it out into the world. We attribute it to all those *others* who are in need of our love, service, and compassion, all the while denying that we ourselves might be in exactly the same condition. Love and care-giving are one-directional. We forego expecting anything in return (that would be self-centered!) and end up of seeing the world as a bottomless pit of need, an image that more honestly applies to our own neglected and repudiated inner state. Is it any wonder that such compassionate caregivers so often end up depressed and burnt out?

What, then, is a psychologically healthier version of compassion?

The "Bodhisattva's Vow," composed by one of Hakuin's disciples, Torei Enji (1721–1792), offers an entirely different vantage point from which to approach the whole idea of compassion. The overarching theme of the vow is one of appreciation and gratitude for the way the world already is: "When I, a student of the Way, look at the real form of the universe, all is the never failing manifestation of the mysterious truth of the Awakened Life."

Our vow is to strive to see the world in this way, as complete and always manifesting the Way. The bodhisattva's compassion is not defined by giving or sacrifice; it is first and foremost a way of seeing. It is only from the proper vantage point that right action can emerge, and that vantage is one that sees the intrinsic wholeness and interconnection of the world, not one that emphasizes what it lacks.

Even though ours is a lay practice center and I am not a priest, I always insist that our zazen is a *religious* practice. For me, this means it is grounded in a sense of reverence and awe for life as it is. Our zazen is not a means to an end, not even a charitable end. Like life, it is complete in and of itself, and it is this perspective we vow to uphold, manifest, and transmit. From this vantage point spontaneously flows "tender care with respectful hearts, / Even to such beings as birds and beasts." Care goes hand in hand with respect, with treating everyone and everything as worthy of our respect.

I remember once when the poet and Zen teacher Philip Whalen came to New York City to give a reading at St Mark's Church. In the courtyard was a statue of Peter Stuyvesant. Whalen stopped in front of the statue and bowed. "Why are you bowing to that old scoundrel?" I asked. "I bow to everything," he replied.

In the imagery of the "Bodhisattva's Vow," the Awakened One, the Buddha, is trying to awaken all beings to the reality of nonseparation, of our intrinsic interconnectedness. He sees that we are sometimes capable of beginning to understand this truth under benign, nonthreatening circumstances. We may feel harmony and oneness within our own community or in relation to nature. But this nascent understanding has its boundaries, and these are typically marked out by and reinforced in the face of suffering. Something is required to push us past our inertial limits, and so the old master suggests Buddha "uses devices" to further awaken us.

Although this language was perhaps taken literally at the level of religious folklore, in the same way in the Judeo-Christian tradition one might speak of God's plan extending down into the particulars of our everyday life, there is a deeper, nontheistic, nonliteral sense to these words as well. At the purely psychological level, we are being told that we can use the experience of being mistreated to remind ourselves of the artificial boundaries we set up in the creation of an Other. Suffering may be the precipitant, but it is also the reminder to attend to our reflexive tendency to split off as not-me that aspect of our common humanity which is now fragmenting into doer and done to. It is precisely in situations of "abuse and persecution" that we are inclined to reflexively devolve into complementarity, to see the world not as manifesting the harmony of the Awakened life but in the black-and-white opposition of self and other.

If ethics may be said to consist, in very large part, in learning to behave well when we are treated badly, both Buddhism and relational psychoanalysis offer perspectives on how to move beyond doer and done to, beyond the endless perpetuation of the cycle of injury, retaliation, and reinjury that characterizes so many conflicts at both the personal and international level. Breaking out of reactive cycles may be a better way of understanding compassion than a picture of endless one-directional giving.

The "Bodhisattva's Vow" is a vivid exhortation to move beyond doer and done to. Within the language of psychoanalysis, we speak of the *Third* as way of representing a perspective that goes beyond these dichotomies. This may be especially challenging when dealing with cases of trauma, or of abuse and persecution, as the verse puts it. Trauma almost inevitably invites us to see the world divided into victims and perpetrators. The traumatized person is defined by what has been *done to* them. Often such individuals feel a sense of passivity and helplessness in the aftermath of trauma.

Furthermore, the world itself is experienced as a passive, unresponsive bystander to their suffering, much the way a child feels when say, the mother fails to notice or act when the father has been an abuser. The child ends up losing both parents; the father as the abuser, but also the mother as the *failed witness*, one who knew but did not act. The goal is restore a sense of agency without resorting to simply changing sides, not succumbing to equating justice with revenge or retribution; the Third, rather, embodies the restoration of a lawful world, one in which suffering is recognized and acknowledged.

As therapists, we cannot undo what has been done. But we can allow the unspeakable to become speakable and to call what has been done by its true name. Sadly, there has too often been a repetition of the scenario of the failed witness in Buddhist communities where abuse has taken place. Whether in the name of preserving the Sangha or the Dharma, or simply protecting the teacher, the truth remains unspoken, the pain never acknowledged, real action never taken. Too often, the wider community of Buddhist teachers has also remained silent, again, failing in its broader responsibility to bear witness.

From both the Buddhist perspective and the perspective of relational analysis, our well-being can never be ours alone and the end of our personal suffering can only be achieved in tandem with resolving our conflicts with others. Like Vimalakirti whose illness cannot be cured until the suffering of all beings is cured, the bodhisattva's vow is as much a description of the nonseparate state as it is an aspiration to it. Compassion has at its core the aspiration to help others awaken. What we awaken to is nonseparation. The bodhisattva recognizes she is nonseparate from all fellow beings; to the extent they are caught in delusive dichotomies, she is as well and her own full liberation cannot take place apart from theirs. We fulfill the vow by over and over affirming our common humanity, our common buddha nature, not by attempting to efface ourselves in the name of a spiritual ideal.

To be ethically meaningful as well as therapeutic, both Buddhism and psychoanalysis must extend their reach beyond the confines of the analytic couch and the meditation cushion. But that move into the world is primarily a move of sharing a vision of that world with others. We are not drained by that sharing and its depth is not measured in terms of our own sacrifice or pain. The joy of realization is the wellspring of compassion, and if we lose touch with that joy in the midst of our seemingly "selfless" giving, we will be a poor impetus indeed for the awakening of anyone else.

CHAPTER TWENTY-ONE

ALIVE OR DEAD

TAO-SHUAI'S THREE BARRIERS

First barrier: Monks, you leave no stone unturned to explore the depths, simply to see into your True Nature. Now I want to ask you, just at this moment: where is your True Nature?

Second barrier: If you realize your True Nature, you are free from life and death. Tell me, when your eyesight deserts you at the last moment, how can you be free from life and death?

Third barrier: When you set yourself free from life and death, you should know your ultimate destination. So when the four elements separate, where will you go?

It is strange that the one thing we all have in common should be something that is also said to be entirely private, the one thing everyone must ultimately do alone. When as psychoanalysts we talk to our patients about their fear of dying, so often it is some aspect of being totally alone that stands out. Patients speak of being cut off from loved ones and from the world, of imaging themselves lost in a void, unable to reach out or communicate, of dissolving or falling apart. Freud maintained that the unconscious does not, cannot imagine the possibility of its own nonexistence and that whenever we try to imagine death, we are always present as a spectator when we envision it. In traditional psychoanalytic terms, what we fear is going to happen to us is always cast in terms of what has already happened to us in the past. Death is thus variously imagined in terms of abandonment, separation, castration (a symbolic stand-in for all sorts of loss of agency), and annihilation (the experience of the self losing cohesion and falling into fragmentation). One of my patients spoke of her anxieties as a feeling like she was losing all her "intermolecular glue," of literally coming apart at the seams.

Thus, part of what we, as psychoanalysts, offer our patients who are facing death is help in moving out of their own isolated fears into a relational world in which fears are mutually known, shared, held, and lived through.

There are a number of koans that illustrate Zen's particular perspective on life and death. Such koans ask us, first and foremost, to clarify "Who dies?" Next, they engage our fantasies of transcendence, our curative fantasies about how, through Zen practice, we might somehow get to a place beyond life and death. And finally they bring us back to the inescapable fact of death itself and what it means to face and experience our death fully.

One story concerns an old master named Tao-wu (Jap. Dogo), who goes with one of his disciples to pay a condolence call to a family where someone has just died. The coffin sits in the middle of the room; the family is gathered around. After performing the requisite chants and rituals, the master is about to leave when his student decides to take this opportunity to get at the heart of the matter. The student goes up to the coffin, bangs it with his fist, and demands to know: "Alive or dead?" The master immediately replies, "I won't say alive; I won't say dead." The student, becoming increasing agitated, grabs the master by his lapels, shakes him, and shouts, "Tell me, alive or dead or I'll hit you." The master says,

"Hit me all you want, but I won't say." The student indeed gives his master a punch and leaves confused and unsatisfied. It should also perhaps be noted that the story doesn't tell us how the family felt about all this carrying on . . .

Not long afterward, old Master Tao-wu himself died. The student, at loose ends, visits another master, tells him the story of what happened, and asks him the same question. The new master looks him straight in the eye and says, "I won't say. I won't say." But this time the monk realized he wasn't being denied an answer; he had in fact been given the answer all along.

What kind of answer is "I won't say"? Buddhism challenges us to dissolve what we imagine are the essential dualisms of existence, dualisms like self and other, or alive and dead. If any dualism could be said to be indisputably true, you would think it would be the difference between alive and dead. Yet the old master asserted that the true nature of what lay in front of him in the coffin was "I won't say." It's not simply *either-or* or even *both-and*. I won't be forced by your question to come down on one side or the other.

How can that be? To understand, we must go back to the fundamental fact that everything is in a state of continuous change. Nothing has a permanent essence or core identity that either exists or doesn't. Buddha taught that the self—but not just the self, everything—the coffin as well as the body in it, are ever changing, one moment always dying into the next. The person I was at age 10 is gone. The person I was at 20, 30, 40, 50, and 60: all are gone. The death of who I am now will not be a discontinuous event unrelated to all those previous passings. My being alive has been inseparable from all those other selves passing away.

Now this paraphrase of the meaning of why we are neither alive or dead is of no use to anyone, any more than hearing that the time after we die will be no different from and need not be any more frightening than the time before we were born. Zen teaches that we have to go through every experience as it comes and that our attempts at any prior understanding are usually nothing but an evasion of the raw, unknowable, uncontrollable reality of whatever is around the next corner.

My old teacher Joko shook her head in dismay when someone asked her about facing death. Even dying, she sighed, is now something people think they have to do well. When you're dying, then you'll find out all you need to know about the subject. If you're afraid of death, then your only option is to go through that fear as honestly as you can and have that experience as well. But having someone by your side to talk about what you fear and where those fears come from is a way of entering and living through those fears more deeply and thoroughly, allowing them to be faced and be something we hold in common.

Another old Zen master, Tao-shuai, challenged his students with the three barrier questions with which this chapter began:

> First barrier: Monks, you leave no stone unturned to explore the depths, simply to see into your True Nature. Now I want to ask you, just at this moment: where is your True Nature?
>
> Second barrier: If you realize your True Nature, you are free from life and death. Tell me, when your eyesight deserts you at the last moment, how can you be free from life and death?
>
> Third barrier: When you set yourself free from life and death, you should know your ultimate destination. So when the four elements separate, where will you go?

These koans hold in dialectical balance two aspects of Zen's teaching about death: on the one hand, the inescapability, the ultimate reality of death as inseparable from our human nature, and on the other the unreality, the emptiness of death in the face of no-self and the emptiness of all existence.

In the Platform Sutra, we read that when the Sixth Patriarch announced to his disciples that he was about to die, all of them broke into tears except Shen-hui. Whereupon Hui-neng declared that it was only he who truly understood his teaching. If we truly understand the emptiness of the self, there is no death and no one who dies. And yet, as Dogen says in Genjokoan, still flowers fall and we are not unmoved by their falling. We can express our understanding either with silence or with unrestrained tears.

As he was dying, Master Lung-t'an cried out, "It hurts, it hurts!" To his students, who were trying to comfort him, Lung-t'an said, "Don't think that my agony now is in any way different from what my joy and exuberance was." Yen-t'ou, being murdered by bandits, let out a great shout. Hakuin, who as a young monk was beset by fears of hell and curative fantasies of imperviousness, was deeply shaken by the story of Yen-t'ou's death and driven to go beyond his longing for transcendence.

How will we pass through Tao-shuai's three barriers?

How will we discover our true nature? Like our original face, has it ever been hidden? Can we find it in the very mind that searches, rather than forever imagining it's somehow eluding our grasp? Can we find true freedom in the very act of dying as did Lung-t'an and Yen-t'ou? And when at last we lie in our coffin, where will we have gone? Will we be alive or dead?

I won't say.

CHAPTER TWENTY-TWO

ENDINGS

BUILD ME A SEAMLESS MONUMENT

The Emperor of China Su-tsung asked national teacher Hui-chung, "What will you need after you die?"

The national teacher said, "Make me a seamless monument."

The Emperor said, "Please tell me what the monument would be like."

The national teacher was silent for a long while. Then he said, "Understand?"

The Emperor said, "I don't understand."

The national teacher said, "I have a disciple to whom I have imparted the teaching, Tan-yuan, who is an expert in this matter. Please ask him."

After the national teacher passed on, the Emperor summoned Tan-yuan and asked him what this meant.

Tan-yuan said, "South of Hsiang, north of T'an—therein is gold sufficient enough for the whole country. Under the shadowless tree is the communal ferryboat; up in the crystal palace there is none who knows."

We end where we began, looking in the mirror, saying this is me. Looking out the window onto the wide world, saying this is me. At the beginning of a traditional psychoanalysis, the patient is told to simply say whatever comes to mind. When, after years of evasion, shame, self-editing, denial, self-criticism, and self-aggrandizement, the patient can finally follow this simple rule, the analysis is over. What do we have to show for all our efforts, all those years of practice? What does it mean to erect a seamless monument as testimony to our realization? Seamless, not being made up of visibly joined parts, would seem to stand for an indivisible oneness or emptiness. A traditional Buddhist memorial is a tower like a pagoda or stupa, divided up into tiers said variously to represent the parts of the Buddha's body or the fundamental elements of earth, water, fire, air, and the void. Are we the sum of our parts, the sum of our history, our accomplishments and failures? Or something more—or something less—than all of that?

The national teacher challenges the Emperor to consider what a life adds up to.

When the Emperor does not understand what a seamless monument means, the master stands before him in silence. Does that silence itself represent seamlessness? It is a great temptation to think so, and one way or another most of us engage in that secret fantasy. We would like our mind swept clean and for it to be as clear as the surface of an unruffled lake. It must have been a temptation in the old days as well, because the Soto master Tenkei (1648–1735) warns in his commentary on this case that "there are no dragons in stagnant water."

In what ways could we imagine our life to be seamless? Perhaps we would like our life to be impeccable, seamless in its virtue. A life of no regrets, no mistakes. Has anyone ever had such a life? Are our lives therefore marred by our failures, our sins staining our soul or our reputation for all time? Is the alternative to whitewash our image, to present a façade of practice or goodness to the world, while pretending to ourselves and others that we have once and for all vanquished our shadow side?

The theme that has run through this book, all the koans, all the psychoanalytic theory, is that we must learn to take ourselves and life whole.

Seamless will have to mean we don't divide our life into the good parts and the bad parts, there is only life, taken whole with all its joy and suffering inextricably intertwined. Our practice, whether in Zen or in psychotherapy, is to discern where we draw the line, so to speak, what divisions we carve into what is intrinsically whole and seamless. We come to say "this is me" with acceptance, not when we have finally, after many years of practice, become the person we always hoped to be, but when we can finally face the person we always have been, the one we are right now.

When it's Tan-yuan's turn to explain his master's wishes to the Emperor, his response is completely different from his old teacher's silence. In many koans, when a student doesn't understand the first time around and seeks a second opinion from another teacher, the second teacher simply repeats the words of the first. But here, Tan-yuan's answer is quite elaborate and poetic. Even if we can't immediately understand what is meant by the references to "South of Hsiang, north of T'an" and so forth, we can see that all this particular detail is just the opposite of silence and what we would ordinarily think of as "seamless." Instead of simplicity, we are offered complexity. Instead of the immediacy of silence (or a shout or a slap) we are offered subtle imagery and extravagant metaphor.

I would suggest that both Hui-chung and Tan-yuan are presenting us with the whole world, but that wholeness is being presented from two different perspectives. Like our duck and rabbit, you can see "seamless" in two very different ways; life as an unbroken whole or life as a vast container for the myriad things. Form is emptiness; emptiness form. Two visions of the same thing.

Not two, not one.

INSIGHT

WASH YOUR BOWLS

Once a monk made a request of Chao-chou. "I have just entered the monastery," he said. "Please give me instruction, Master." Chao-chou said, "Have you had your breakfast?" "Yes, I have," replied the monk. "Then," said Chao-chou, "wash your bowls."

What do we come away with after years of practice? What do we come away with after reading—or writing—a book about Zen? What kind of insights do we hope to achieve or pass on?

Insight is a concept central to both Zen and psychoanalysis. Both offer practices that promise a way to see through a veil of misunderstanding, whether that veil is itself understood to exist as a result of delusions or psychological defenses. On the other side of that veil is what? "Life as it is," was the way my teacher put it. Freud, speaking as the scientist he thought himself, might have said simply, "reality."

However, insight in neither Zen nor therapy can be merely a matter of revealing a hidden truth. The process, the practice itself, embodies the final lesson. The monk in this koan thinks insight is something to have, to possess, the way he had oatmeal for breakfast. Chao-chou offers him the corrective that insight may mean taking something away, not adding something on top of what we already have. Washing our bowls, we let go of any notion of having something to show for our efforts. Our hunger, our craving, is gone; what we're left with are dirty dishes. Nothing to be proud of, just something to be dealt with in the everyday way of such things.

What we experience, what is revealed to us in analysis and Zen, is not something that can be passed on in words to someone else. The insight that I never felt loved is no more transferable than the realization that everything I see is nothing other than myself. Unlike scientific truths, these insights must be renewed individually over and over again from one generation to the next. In that sense, there cannot be progress in religious or psychological practices the way there is in science.

The setting and styles of practice may evolve, and there may now be fewer Buddhists who are homeless mendicants just as there are fewer analysands lying a couch five days a week. Yet, in some important sense, individual patients or meditators must recapitulate within themselves the history of their respective practice. We must convince ourselves anew that our minds are not as open and transparent to our introspection as we have thought; we must see that processes are taking place out of our usual awareness that allow us to avoid painful inner emotional territory and to construct elaborate unconscious narratives that add up to my "self" and my world. We must place our selves in a practice and relational setting in which we are both actor and acted upon; allowing experiences to emerge in these new contexts that we would have hitherto labeled as "not-me."

Finally, we must come to realize that the insights we achieve in our respective practices are not solvents that dissolve our suffering and our self-centeredness in a once-and-for-all kind of manner. Dropping off body and mind must be reenacted in zazen endlessly, and as Kodo Sawaki insisted, the dropping off of body-mind is inseparable from the activity of zazen. Our psychological insights can deliver us from being frozen in an inner world of self-hate, but our characters will quickly congeal if the insight is not exercised every day thereafter. No amount of insight (on the couch or on the cushion) into the origins of our overeating, drinking, compulsive or avoidant behaviors will make the habits of a lifetime simply dissolve.

As the old beat poet Gregory Corso once observed, "Rome wasn't burnt in a day." We are freed only to the extent that we continually live against the grain of those old habits, and only by so living do we gain the new experiences that can gradually disconfirm those deeply held beliefs about what can keep us safe or satisfied.

Zen, like any religious practice, or like yoga and many forms of healthful exercise, is a lifelong practice. In order to transform our lives, disciplines like zazen must be practiced *religiously*, and to practice something religiously, it helps to have a religion. Psychotherapy is still looking for ways to understand and justify some equivalent version of lifelong self-inquiry. Arising within the context of a medical model, therapy has traditionally been conceived of as part of a time-limited sequence of illness, treatment, and termination.

Sometimes a chronic illness will require a lifetime of treatment or maintenance therapy. But within the mental health community, an unending psychotherapy is usually spoken of in a fashion that is either perjorative (i.e., the analyst fostering dependency for his own narcissistic needs) or pathologizing (e.g., the patient being so regressed or dysfunctional as to not be able to stand on his own two feet). Within the broader field of psychotherapeutic approaches, cognitive behavior therapies exemplify a countervailing trend toward short-term psychotherapy.

Ten sessions of therapy, like a single week-long sesshin, may indeed yield what feel like life-changing insights, but I believe it is the rare individual who successfully transforms her life as a result.

Moreover, I am quite comfortable with the idea of someone trying short-term therapy or psychotropic medication before coming to psychoanalysis (or Zen)—solve what can be solved that way, then come talk to me about the rest.

Even within psychoanalysis, the metaphors of growth, development, and separation hold sway in way that can dovetail with the medical model's goal of cure and termination. The baby starts out totally dependent on the mother, but her care leads to the child's increasing capacity for independence and ultimate separation.

What alternative metaphors are possible?

Perhaps, within the developmental model, we can shift away from the picture of the infant separating and individuating or the adolescent becoming an adult and leaving home. Perhaps we can also consider the relationship of adult children to their parents, which is lifelong. Are there other metaphors like this that would respect rather than pathologize lifelong attachment and an open-ended analytic relationship? We don't speak of a need to mature and separate from our Zen teacher or rabbi, though maybe here psychoanalysis can help us sort out pathological dependency from devotion.

Can bringing together these two disciplines help us rethink whether they have the trajectory we have always assumed? The process of becoming Zen teacher and receiving Dharma transmission is a long and unpredictable path, quite unlike entering medical school, which has a predetermined time frame and an almost guaranteed outcome upon completion. Can, or should, Dharma teaching be professionalized?

Teachers could certainly use training in the psychological, interpersonal, and group processes. The economics of teaching and running a center or monastery is a subject too little discussed. A preoccupation with fundraising and the reliance of many centers on the largesse of a few wealthy donors can create tensions in a sangha that are hard to acknowledge or resolve. More and more sanghas are developing more democratic decision-making processes and their governing boards are in recent years less prone to be rubber stamps for the teacher.

America does not have a tradition of family-run temples or of centralized training monasteries. Lay practice is coming out of the shadow of the monastic ideal and represents a new path for practice, training, and transmission of the Dharma. Above all, we are beginning to recognize the importance of pace and sustainability to a lifelong practice. We need styles of practice that support and strengthen our relationships, marriages, and families. The old model of home-leaving shouldn't translate for us as home-wrecking. This is a lesson that I, and many of my generation, learned the hard way.

For many of us—as teachers, as clinicians, as patients, and as practitioners—the boundaries between disciplines of self-care, the therapeutic, and the spiritual are both ambiguous and porous. In classical Western culture, the role of the philosopher, paradigmatically exemplified by Socrates, was to lead his interlocutors into a dialogue about the nature of the good life. In the generations following Socrates, schools of Stoics, Skeptics, and Epicurians, each in its own way, evolved what philosopher Martha Nussbaum called "therapies of desire," a term that would seem to fit aspects of Buddhism as well as psychoanalysis.

But the public role of the philosopher himself has dropped out of the picture, and his function has bifurcated into two separate paths, the therapeutic and the spiritual. Much of what now goes on within the ostensibly medical or therapeutic discipline of psychoanalysis and psychotherapy involves confronting existential issues of identity, meaning, and mortality. Many therapists are themselves turning to one form of meditation practice or another as a way of ongoing self-exploration and self-care. Meanwhile, within Zen and other spiritual practices, teachers are confronted with students hoping for relief from anxiety, depression, and addictive behaviors.

The integration of these two paths is thus not so much a matter of integrating techniques from different disciplines as it is a matter of acknowledging how goals and functions that we are used to thinking about separately are becoming increasingly mixed together, in ways that raise the expectations placed on each, often resulting in confusion and disappointment. All too often, students and teachers have become entangled in transferential and dissociative processes that traditional Buddhist psychology and Zen practice has failed to address.

I have tried to show how a relational psychoanalytic approach can help us understand the origin of these entanglements. The process of building conceptual and experiential bridges between Zen Buddhism and psychoanalysis has lagged behind the connections being forged between mindfulness based meditation techniques and cognitive behavioral therapy. I have tried to show what new perspectives can be opened up by taking a psychoanalytically oriented approach.

Throughout this book I have linked the understanding of koans to an understanding of the underlying psychological issues that stand in the way of our appreciating the vistas the old masters were trying to share with us. We will be unable to participate in the oneness of all existence if we are unable to experience the totality of our own selves. Splitting off and disowning aspects of our self, we create a damaged, divided world in which we strive after an elusive transcendental wholeness.

Everything we seek is hidden in plain sight. Reality, life as it is, displays itself totally to us moment after moment, even though we usually can see only one of its faces at a time. The more we grow in our capacity to see and acknowledge all parts of our self, the more we are able to see the perfection that manifests all around, a perfection that does not erase or negate the brokenness and suffering of the world, but which is nonetheless always there, the face of the duck smiling out from where before we were only able to see the ears of a rabbit.

NOTES

I have drawn from many different sources and translations for the koans discussed in this book, some of which substitute the Japanese version of a master's name for the original Chinese (i.e., Joshu for Chao-chou). In the interest of uniformity, I have used the Wade-Giles version of the Chinese names throughout, regardless of which appears in the original source.

INTRODUCTION

"Beginning with Nishiari Zenji's..." K. Yamada, "The Stature of Yasutani Hak-uun Roshi," in *Eastern Buddhist*, n.s., 7.2 (1974): 119. Cited on DharmaWeb.org.

"The zazen I speak of..." Dogen, *Fukanzazenji*, in R. Aitken and K. Tanahashi (2000), *Enlightenment Unfolds*.

"There's another man within me, and he's angry with me." Graham Greene, echoing Thomas Browne, in the epigraph to his first novel, *Brighton Rock*. Quoted in P. Iyer (2012), *The Man Within My Head*, 50.

CHAPTER ONE

Stephen Batchelor has attempted to reconstruct what can be known about the historical Buddha in *Confessions of a Buddhist Atheist* (2011).

"In the heavens above, and in the four quarters of the earth, there is none holier than I." S. Ogata (1990), *Transmission of the Lamp*, 4.

"For the first three years he practiced the samadhi (deep meditation) of non-action..." Ibid.

"...this thing of darkness I / Acknowledge mine." W. Shakespeare, *The Tempest*, Act V, scene I.

CHAPTER TWO

Portions of this chapter originally appeared in *The Book of Mu*, edited by James Ford (2011).

The story of Junpo Kelly and the Dalai Lama can be found in K. Martin-Smith (2012), *A Heart Blown Open: The Life & Practice of Zen Master Jun Po Denis Kelly Roshi*, 276.

CHAPTER THREE

"Pray, Master, of your mercy, allow me to beg you for the teaching of emancipation." Ogata (1990), 81.

"The law of inescapability" and direct quotes by Jessica Benjamin (1998) are from *The Shadow of the Other: Intersubjectivity and Gender in Psychoanalysis*, 102–5.

"...desire [that] is actually an obstacle..." Lauren Berlant (2011), *Cruel Optimism*, 1.

CHAPTER FOUR

All the quotes from Hakuin's autobiography are taken from Norman Waddell's 1999 translation.

Shohaku Okamura's story (2012) is told in *Living by Vow*, 182–84.

Nantembo (1839–1925) was the Dharma nickname of Toshu Zenchu, who was known for his challenging style and for carrying a "nantembo," a big stick. Another one of his scrolls, illustrating his stick, is inscribed, "If you can answer, I'll give you a hundred blows; if you cannot answer, one hundred blows."

The teachings of Bankei are collected in Normal Waddell, trans. (2000), *The Unborn: The Life and Teachings of Zen Master Bankei*.

Chao-chou (Jap. Joshu) answering "no" to one monk and "yes" to another can be found in case 18 of *The Book of Serenity* (Hudson, NY: Lindisfarne Press, 1990).

CHAPTER FIVE

Huang-po's (Jap. Obaku) "Gobblers of Dregs" is Blue Cliff Record, case 11: "I do not say that there is no Zen, it's just that there are no teachers."

My description of the Third is drawn primarily from Jessica Benjamin's (2004) *Beyond Doer and Done To: An Intersubjective View of Thirdness.*

CHAPTER SIX

"...some scholars have insinuated..." See particularly A. Cole (2009), *Fathering Your Father: The Zen of Fabrication in Tang Buddhism.*

"...attributed to Confucius..." See J. Jorgensen (2012), "The Figure of Huineng," in M. Schlutter and S. Teiser (Eds.), *Readings of the Platform Sutra.*

"The time has probably come..." Thomas Merton (1997), *Dancing in the Water of Life*, 9.

CHAPTER SEVEN

"A monk asked Ta-lung..." The Blue Cliff Record, case 82.

"...not 'mere' appearances..." I owe this description to Terry Eagleton's (2009) explication of the philosophy of Bishop Berkeley: "The great secret that Berkeley triumphantly lays bare, in the manner of the child artlessly announcing the nakedness of the Emperor, is that what the appearances of things is concealing is the fact that there is nothing behind them; that they are consequently not appearances at all; and that this hard core we call 'substance' is as flimsy as fantasy.... To say things lack substance is to say they are the eloquent discourse of the divine. God—sheer nothingness—is of their essence" (81).

"A radical shift in perspective..." Stephen Batchelor (2011), *Confessions of a Buddhist Atheist*, 129.

the unattributed drawing of the duck-rabbit first appeared as "Kaninchen und Ente" ("Rabbit and Duck") in the October 23, 1892, issue of *Fliegende Blätter.*

CHAPTER EIGHT

Shohaku Okamura (2012) on transmigration: "Many people believe in transmigration from one lifetime to another. I don't believe this but I know we transmigrate within this life" (135).

The story of the encounter between Dickens and Dostoyevsky is taken from the *New York Times* review by Michiko Kakutani of *Charles Dickens* by Claire Tomalin, Oct 24, 2011. If this story sounds too good to be true, it probably is. Eric Naiman has recently determined that Dickens's biographer was the victim of an elaborate literary hoax that fabricated the story of this encounter.

The expression "Wherever you go, there you are" was used as a book title by Jon Kabat-Zinn in 1995. However, the origin of the phrase is murky and an internet search finds it in both Thomas à Kempis and Confucius.

CHAPTER NINE

This translation of the main case is taken from Shibayama Roshi's (1974) *Zen Comments on the Mumonkan*. The lines from Wu-men's verse are the version in Robert Aitken's (1991) *The Gateless Barrier*.

"a failure of responsiveness..." Philip Bromberg (2006), *Awakening the Dreamer*, 139–40.

"Analysts have learned that they must own the attribution of retraumatizing the patient..." A discussion of this issue can be found in Jessica Benjamin's (2009) "A Relational Psychoanalysis Perspective on the Necessity of Acknowledging Failure in order to Restore the Facilitating and Containing Features of the Intersubjective Relationship (the Shared Third)."

The three ancient witches of Greek mythology were called the Graeae, and they shared one eye and one tooth among them. By snatching their single eye while they were in the midst of passing it, the hero Perseus was able to force them to tell him how he could defeat the monster Medusa.

CHAPTER TEN

Ma-tu's Sun-faced Buddha, Moon-faced Buddha: The Blue Cliff Record, case 3.

See Mary Beard (2012), "Do the Classics Have a Future?"

"I can think of only one..." Carolyn Atkinson, personal communication.

CHAPTER ELEVEN

The initial quotes from are Joko Beck's (1989) *Everyday Zen*, 72.

This version of the story of the old woman and the hermit is taken from case 162 in the Rinzai koan collection *Shumon Kattoshu* ("Entangled Vines"), translated by Thomas Kirchner (2004),84.

Ezra Pound's "Song in the Manner of Housman" originally appeared in Canzoni's 1911 collection. It is reprinted from E. Pound (1972), *Collected Early Poems*, with permission of New Directions.

The quote from Dan Siegel (1999) is from *The Developing Mind*, 172.

An excellent summary of the work of Bowlby, Ainsworth, and the development of attachment theory can be found in Robert Karen's (1998) *Becoming Attached*, from which my description of the Strange Situation experiments is drawn.

The account of different babies' attachment styles is taken from R. Karen (1998), *Becoming Attached*, 161.

CHAPTER TWELVE

This account of intersubjectivity differs from that given in chapter five's discussion of the Third. Both Stolorow and Benjamin use the word "intersubjectivity" to describe aspects of our essential interconnectedness. However, as is often the case with psychoanalysts from different theoretical lineages, they use the word in significantly different ways, sometimes leading to confusion and questions of priority. For Stolorow, intersubjectivity is the state in which we all automatically exist; there can be, from the moment of birth, no such thing as an isolated mind. Benjamin, in contrast, uses intersubjectivity to refer to the specific developmental achievement of recognition of the other as a separate subjectivity.

The myth of the isolated mind is described in Stolorow and Atwood (1992), 9–11.

"If a lion could talk…" Wittgenstein (1953), *Philosophical Investigations*, 223; "Am I less certain…" Ibid., 224.

The encounter between Errol Morris and Thomas Kuhn is taken from "The Ashtray: An Ultimatum," *New York Times Online*, March 6, 2011.

CHAPTER THIRTEEN

The discussion of cell boundaries is taken from H. Maturana and F. Varela (1987), *The Tree of Knowledge*.

"The practice of acceptance…" C. Atkinson (2010), *A Light in the Mind: Living Your Life Just As It Is*, 81.

Kuei-shan (Jap. Isan) and Liu (Jap. Ryutetsema): The Book of Equanimity, case 60.

CHAPTER FOURTEEN

Hsueh-feng (Jap. Seppo) the Rice Cook: The Book of Equanimity, case 55.

CHAPTER FIFTEEN

Feng-hsueh's Speech and Silence: Wu-men kuan, case 24; translation by Miura and Sasaki (1966).

The traditional system of classifying koans is described in Miura and Sasaki's (1966) *Zen Dust*, where case 24 from the Wu-men kuan is used as an example of a *gonsen* koan, one dealing with the use of language. My own training did not include such systematic koan study.

"do not describe or report..." J. L. Austin (1975), *Doing Things with Words*, 5.

The mereological fallacy—the confusion of parts with wholes—is discussed at length in Bennett and Hacker (2003), *Philosophical Foundations of Neuroscience*.

Morgenbesser's immortal quip at Austin's lecture at Columbia was prominently featured in his obituary in the *New York Times*, August 4, 2004.

Marianne Moore's (1951) line about "imaginary gardens with real toads in them" is from a poem titled "Poetry."

CHAPTER SIXTEEN

Pai-chang (Jap. Hyakujo) and the Fox: Wu-men kuan, case 2.

CHAPTER SEVENTEEN

"Zazen is not a meditation technique..." Dogen, *Fukanzazengi*. This translation is by Uchiyama Roshi and comes from the website of Antaiji monastery.

"To study the buddha way is to study the self...." Aitken and Tanahashi (2000).

CHAPTER EIGHTEEN

"My feeling had always been..." Bernie Glassman, interview, on the website "Sweeping Zen," April 24, 2012.

Hui-neng called "into question the sequentialist understanding of precepts, meditation and wisdom." Groner (2012), "Ordination and Precepts in the Platform Sutra," 152.

The quotation from Suzuki Roshi is taken from Michael Wenger's (1994) modern koan collection *Thirty-Three Fingers*.

CHAPTER NINETEEN

Tung-shan's (Jap. Tozan) No Heat or Cold: The Blue Cliff Record, case 43.

Thomas Merton's ongoing conflicts with the Church hierarchy are documented in Mott's (1984) biography.

The quotes from Ghent on submission and surrender are taken from "Masochism, Submission, Surrender: Masochism as a Perversion of Surrender," *Contemporary Psychoanalysis* 26: 108–36.

A discussion of the psychodynamic issues raised by *The Story of O* can be found in Jessica Benjamin's (1988) *The Bonds of Love*.

CHAPTER TWENTY

This version of the "Bodhisattva's Vow," a composite of a number of translations, is the one currently in use at the Ordinary Mind Zendo.

Peter Stuyvesant (1612–1672) was the director of New Amsterdam, the precursor of present-day New York City. He was an autocratic leader who persecuted the Quakers and Jews living under his jurisdiction.

CHAPTER TWENTY-ONE

My paraphrase of Master Tao-wu's (Jap. Dogo) "Alive or Dead" is taken from the Blue Cliff Record, case 55.

Tao-shuai's Three Barriers: The Gateless Barrier, case 47.

The story of Mater Lung-t'an (Jap. Ryutan) is cited in Richard Shrobe's (2010) *Elegant Failure: A Guide to Zen Koans*, 190.

CHAPTER TWENTY-TWO

"The Emperor of China..." T. Cleary (2000), *Secrets of the Blue Cliff Record*, case 18. The expression "South of Sho, north of Tan" does refer to the whole world, from one end to the other.

"there are no dragons in stagnant water." Cleary (2000), 60.

CONCLUSION

This version of the koan is taken from Shibayama Roshi's (1974) *Zen Comments on the Mumonkan*, case 7.

REFERENCES

Aitken, R., & Tanahashi, K. (2000). *Enlightenment Unfolds*. Boston: Shambhala.

Atkinson, C. (2010). *A Light in the Mind: Living Your Life Just As It Is*. Santa Cruz: Everyday Dharma Center.

Austin, J. L. (1975). *How to Do Things with Words*. Cambridge, MA: Harvard University Press.

Batchelor, S. (2011). *Confessions of a Buddhist Atheist*. New York: Random House.

Beard, M. (2012). Do the Classics Have a Future? *New York Review of Books* LIX (1), 49–54.

Beauvoir, S. (1952). *The Second Sex*. New York: Knopf.

Beck, C. (1989). *Everyday Zen*. San Francisco: Harper & Row.

Benjamin, J. (1988). *The Bonds of Love*. New York: Pantheon.

Benjamin, J. (1998). *Shadow of the Other: Intersubjectivity and Gender in Psychoanalysis*. New York: Routledge.

Benjamin, J. (2004). "Beyond Doer and Done To: An Intersubjective View of Thirdness." *Psychoanalytic Quarterly* 73:5–46.

Benjamin, J. (2009). A Relational Psychoanalysis Perspective on the Necessity of Acknowledging Failure in order to Restore the Facilitating and Containing Features of the Intersubjective Relationship (the Shared Third). *International Journal of Psycho-Analysis* 90, 441–50.

Bennett, M. R., & Hacker, P. M. S. (2003). *Philosophical Foundations of Neuroscience*. Oxford: Blackwell.

Berlant, L. (2011). *Cruel Optimism*. Durham, NC: Duke University Press.

Bromberg, P. (2006). *Awakening the Dreamer*. Mahwah, NJ: Analytic Press.

Buber, M. (1991). *Tales of the Hasidim, Book One: The Early Masters* and *Book Two: The Later Masters*. New York: Schocken.

Cleary, T. (2000). *Secrets of the Blue Cliff Record: Zen Comments by Hakuin and Tenkei*. Boston: Shambhala.

Cole, A. (2009). *Fathering Your Father: The Zen of Fabrication in Tang Buddhism*. Berkeley: University of California Press.

Eagleton, T. (2009). *Trouble with Strangers: A Study of Ethics*. Oxford: Wiley-Blackwell.

Flanagan, O. (2007). *The Really Hard Problem: Meaning in a Material World*. Cambridge, MA: MIT Press.

Ford, J. (Ed.). (2011). *The Book of Mu*. Boston: Wisdom.

Freud, S. (1971). Jokes and Their Relation to the Unconscious. In *Standard Edition of the Complete Psychological Works of Sigmund Freud*, Volume VIII. London: Hogarth Press. (Originally published 1905.)

Ghent, E. (1990). Masochism, Submission, Surrender: Masochism as a Perversion of Surrender. *Contemporary Psychoanalysis 26*, 108–36.

Glassman, B. (2012, April 24). Interview. "Sweeping Zen" website. Retrieved February 23, 2013: http://sweepingzen.com/bernie-glassman-interview/.

Groner, P. (2012). Ordination and Precepts in the Platform Sutra. In M. Schlutter & S. Teiser (Eds.). *Readings of the Platform Sutra*. New York: Columbia University Press.

Hui-neng (2006). *The Platform Sutra: The Zen Teaching of Hui-neng* (Red Pine, Trans.). Berkeley: Counterpoint.

Hakuin (1999). *Wild Ivy: The Spiritual Autobiography of Zen Master Hakuin* (N. Waddell, Trans.). Boston: Shambhala.

Iyer, P. (2012). *The Man Within My Head*. New York: Knopf.

Jorgensen, J. (2012). The Figure of Hui-neng. In M. Schlutter & S. Teiser (Eds.). *Readings of the Platform Sutra*. New York: Columbia University Press.

Karen, R. (1998). *Becoming Attached*. New York: Oxford University Press.

Kirchner, T. (2004). *Entangling Vines: Zen Koans of the Shumon Kattoshu*. Kyoto: Tenryu-ji Institute for Philosophy and Religion.

Kohut, H. (1985). *Self Psychology and the Humanities: Reflections on a New Psychoanalytic Approach*. New York: W.W. Norton.

Levinas, E. (1998). *Otherwise than Being*. Pittsburgh: Duquesne University Press.

Loy, D. (2010). *The World Is Made of Stories*. Boston: Wisdom.

Martin-Smith, K. (2012). *A Heart Blown Open: The Life & Practice of Zen Master Jun Po Denis Kelly Roshi*. Studio City, CA: Divine Arts.

Maturana, H., & Varela, F. (1987). *The Tree of Knowledge*. Boston: New Science Library.

Merton, T. (1997). *Dancing in the Water of Life*. New York: Harper Collins.

Mitchell, S. (2000). *Relationality*. Hillsdale, NJ: Analytic Press.

Miura, I., & Sasaki, R. F. (1966). *Zen Dust*. New York: Harcourt, Brace and World.

Moore, M. (1951). *Collected Poems*. New York: Macmillan.

Morris, E. (2011, March 6). The Ashtray: An Ultimatum. *New York Times Online;* Retrieved February 21, 2013: http://opinionator.blogs.nytimes.com/2011/03/06/the-ashtray-the-ultimatum-part-1/.

Mott, M. (1984). *The Seven Mountains of Thomas Merton*. New York: Houghton Mifflin.

Naiman, E. (2013) When Dickens Met Dostoevsky. *Times Literary Supplement* April, 10, 2013.

Okamura, S. (2012). *Living by Vow: A Practical Introduction to Eight Essential Zen Chants and Texts*. Boston: Wisdom.

Ogata, S. (Trans.). (1990). *The Transmission of the Lamp: Early Masters*. Wolfeboro, NH: Longwood.

Pound, E. (1976). *Collected Early Poems*. New York: New Directions.

Rorty, R. (1967). *The Linguistic Turn: Recent Essays in Philosophical Method*. Chicago: University of Chicago Press.

Shibayama, Z. (1974). *Zen Comments on the Mumomkan*. New York: Harper & Row.

Shigematsu, S. (Trans.). (1981). *A Zen Forest: Sayings of the Masters*. New York: Weatherhill.

Shrobe, R. (2010). *Elegant Failure: A Guide to Zen Koans*. Berkeley: Rodmell Press.

Siegel, D. (1999). *The Developing Mind*. New York: Guilford Press.

Stolorow, R., and Atwood, G. (1992). *Contexts of Being: The Intersubjective Foundations of Psychological Life*. Hillsdale, NJ: Analytic Press.

Waddell, N. (Trans.). (2000). *The Unborn: The Life and Teachings of Zen Master Bankei*. Berkeley: North Point.

Watts, A. (1959). *Beat Zen, Square Zen and Zen*. San Francisco: City Lights.

Weschler, L. (1982). *Seeing Is Forgetting the Name of the Thing One Sees*. Berkeley: University of California Press.

Wenger, M. (1994). *Thirty-Three Fingers: A Collection of Modern American Koans*. San Francisco: Clear Glass.

Wittgenstein, L. (1922). *Tractatus Logico-Philosophicus*. London: Kegan Paul.

Wittgenstein, L. (1953). *Philosophical Investigations*. (G.E.M. Anscombe, Trans.). New York: Macmillan.

INDEX

ABOUT THE AUTHOR

 Barry Magid is a psychiatrist and psychoanalyst in New York City. He received his MD from the New Jersey College of Medicine in 1975 and completed his psychoanalytic training at the Postgraduate Center for Mental Health in 1981. He is currently a faculty member and supervisor at The Stephen Mitchell Center for Relational Studies and the Institute for Contemporary Psychotherapy in New York and a member of the Executive Board of the International Associational for Relational Psychoanalysis and Psychotherapy (IARPP). He has published numerous articles within the psychoanalytic field of self psychology and is the editor of *Freud's Case Studies: Self Psychological Perspectives* and the author of *Ordinary Mind: Exploring the Common Ground of Zen and Psychotherapy* and *Ending the Pursuit of Happiness: A Zen Guide.*

From 1989 to 2000, he handprinted books at the Center for Books Arts in New York City and published limited editions of works by Wendell Berry, Guy Davenport, Mark Doty, Jonathan Greene, Jim Harrison, James Laughlin, Thomas Merton, Robert Stone, Charles Tomlinson, Jonathan Williams, William Carlos Williams, and others under the imprint of the Dim Gray Bar Press. His own translation of *Diogenes Laertius*, "Life of Zeno," was published by Larkspur Press in 1996. He also is the editor of *Father Louie: Photographs of Thomas Merton* by Ralph Eugene Meatyard.

In 1996, Charlotte Joko Beck gave him permission to establish the Ordinary Mind Zendo as an affiliate of the San Diego Zen Center and to serve as its teacher. He received Dharma transmission from her in 1999. He is committed to the ongoing integration of the practices of psychodynamic psychotherapy and Zen.

He is one of the founding teachers of the Lay Zen Teachers Association (LZTA), which was established in 2010 and is dedicated to the principle that the Dharma can be fully realized, expressed, and transmitted in the context of lay life.

ABOUT WISDOM PUBLICATIONS

Wisdom Publications is dedicated to offering works relating to and inspired by Buddhist traditions.

To learn more about us or to explore our other books, please visit our website at www.wisdompubs.org.

You can subscribe to our e-newsletter or request our print catalog online, or by writing to:

Wisdom Publications
199 Elm Street
Somerville, Massachusetts 02144 USA

You can also contact us at 617-776-7416,
or info@wisdompubs.org.

Wisdom is a nonprofit, charitable 501(c)(3) organization, and donations in support of our mission are tax deductible.

Wisdom Publications is affiliated with the Foundation for the Preservation of the Mahayana Tradition (FPMT).